May the life, ministry and legacy of my dear sweetie/wife be an inspiration and blessing to all who read this.

God Bless,

Sal   II Tim. 2:15

August 14, 2014

God's Blessed Angel

Compiled By
Robert "Bob" Fraumann

God's Blessed Angel
Published by Yawn's Publishing
198 North Street
Canton, GA 30114
www.yawnspublishing.com

Library of Congress Control Number: 2014937867

ISBN13: 978-1-940395-32-6 paperback
          978-1-940395-33-3 eBook

Printed in the United States

Table of Contents

Witness

Family and Relationships

Celebration and Remembrances

Blessings

Janice
"God's Gracious Gift"

Yet the Lord longs to be gracious to you;
he rises to show you compassion.
For the Lord is a God of justice.
Blessed are all who wait for him!
Isaiah 30:18

Marie
"Living Fragrance"

I praise you because I am fearfully
and wonderfully made; your works are
wonderful, I know that full well.
How precious to me are your thoughts,
O God! How vast is the sum of them!
Psalm 139:14, 17

Janice (Jan) Marie Brown Fraumann

"God's gracious gift."
She surely was that to everyone.

A Woman of Influence

Strength and dignity are her clothing,
and she smiles at the future.
She opens her mouth in wisdom,
and the teaching of kindness
is on her tongue.
You are the light of the world.
Let your light shine...
that they may see your good deeds
and praise your Father in heaven.
God through us spreads everywhere
the fragrance of the knowledge of him.

Proverbs 31:25-28 NASB; Mt. 5:14,16; 2 Corinthians 2:14 NIV

Introduction

This is the story of a unique life, lived with God – just as she lived it with me, her family, her friends, her new acquaintances, or with you (if you were one of the fortunate to have had a personal encounter with Jan, anytime or anywhere).

She would talk, listen or pray with anyone on the spot, always turning the conversation to you, even though she may be the one you came to pray with and bless. My dear friend, Lee Baxley, said that Jan was the epitome of ministry, so this book is not just a biography, but a celebration of her ministry. My prayer is that each of us follows her example.

Jan lived an exciting life of seventy-five years. And, yes, it did have its challenges with polio at the age of twelve. Her left side was paralyzed. She was told she would never live a normal life and never have children. But, she prayed and gave her life to God and He healed her in a year. She lived an incredibly wonderful and fulfilled life.

She started "Jan's Wedding Catering" business and learned to bake wedding cakes on her own. She prepared the finger foods and arranged the flowers. Sometimes she would sing at the wedding and I would play the organ. We used to joke that we did everything but "tie the knot."

Jan and I were privileged to be selected to speak at a Senate Sub Committee in Washington, D.C. As small business owners, we were defending our status, and all other business owners in America, concerning a new law to eliminate tax advantages to business owners.

Jan, along with me, was an incredibly inspiring motivational speaker and teacher across the United States and the Caribbean.

She owned and operated a credit business for twelve years that employed up to ten people and helped provide credit for those who had no credit or bad credit. She was always looking for ways to help people physically as well as spiritually.

Jan sang a solo for the Soroptimist Club (largest women's service organization in the world) in Columbus, Georgia when Jimmy Carter was guest speaker during his run for governor of Georgia.

We had the privilege of meeting several Presidents of the United States, including President Ronald Reagan and President George H.W. Bush. We planned all the music for President Reagan at a rally in Atlanta. As a thank you, we were invited to the White House six months later to meet again with President Reagan.

To Jan Fraumann
With best wishes. Ronald Reagan

Bob, Jan and President Bush

Jan sang a duet with John Davidson in Las Vegas and met Jim Nabors (Gomer). We shared the stage at various motivational and training seminars and met Mary Lou Retton, Jeff Foxworthy, Zig Ziglar, Rich DeVos, Glen Campbell, Vice President Dan Quayle, Phil Driscoll, Dave Thomas, Barbara Mandrell, Robert Schuller, and the list goes on and on.

From 1981 to 1983, Jan and I traveled two weeks out of every month speaking and visiting twenty-four islands in twenty-four months from Hawaii to Bermuda and throughout the Caribbean to South America.

At the end of her life, she contracted cancer beginning at age sixty-five until her death at the age of seventy-five. After ten years of cancer in her leg and breast, and an amputation of her "good leg", not her polio leg, Jan experienced the ultimate healing, as her former pastor, Rev. Tom Pilgrim said, "by taking her to her reward in heaven."

Just before Jan left this earth, she called together all sixteen of her immediate family members at home to pray a special, individual blessing on each of us. With one lung full of pneumonia and cancer and the other lung half full, she laboriously prayed for everyone at least five minutes, praying a special blessing on each of us.

No doubt, it was a glorious trip on August 12, 2013 at 6:20 p.m., as a double rainbow appeared (see book cover) immediately in the sky, symbolizing her arrival in heaven, overcoming victoriously two dreaded diseases, polio and cancer. I know she heard her Lord say, "Welcome, good and faithful servant, enter thou into the joy of your Lord!"

Sometimes I jokingly say, "Some people bring sunshine wherever they go, and some people bring sunshine whenever they go." Another way to say it is, "The room lights up when they walk in, or the room lights up when they walk out." Now the real question is, "What kind of person are you and I?" We all know what kind of a person Jan was!

I know this is a joking way to describe Jan about a very serious subject, but nevertheless it is true. The point is that Jan was a very special lady who had an extremely intimate, special relationship with her Lord, and everyone who experienced her experienced the Lord.

I have witnessed Jan's personal growth with her Lord over many years – fifty-six beautiful years of marriage and two years before that during our dating and engagement.

This was a gradual, deepening experience with Him, during which she loved to spend hours alone with Him, praying, listening, and studying. She loved to study the Word. She loved this personal, quiet time with her Lord. Second Timothy 2:15, "Study to shew thyself approved unto God, a workman that needeth not to be ashamed, rightly dividing the word of truth." We must make time for God. She did! Each of us has a God shaped hole in our heart that only God can fill. He certainly filled Jan's heart completely!

In 1860, the hymn, "Take Time To Be Holy" was written by William D. Longstaff. Even over 150 years ago, people were so busy they had to take time (make time daily) for God. Jan did!

When Jan was with people, individually, in a group, or in a Bible study, they sensed they were in the presence of a saint. When she spoke or shared, everyone automatically focused and listened intently to absorb all she had to say. It was like God speaking directly through her to each of us. Jan certainly lived a life that will outlast her.

Jan journaled over three hundred pages of her journey with God in a sixteen year period from 1991-2007. She made time regularly to do so. However, if she missed a day, God would remind her that He missed this time with her and that He had looked forward to it.

I share in this book (Chapter 5) excerpts of these incredible, fabulous conversations with God (all in quotes). These were sixteen years in her life, before and during cancer. This was her loving, learning, private, rare time with her Lord, usually 4:00 A.M. Samples of these conversations with God are included in the chapter entitled Conversations with God.

I share with you now "the rest of the story" of a life well lived, victoriously and with passion with her Lord.

I like to visualize her writing feverishly as God spoke to her. Please get caught up with these rare moments, as God speaks and Jan writes.

There are seven chapters in this book on the blessing. Many of these excerpts are from the Bible study she taught.

So why this book?

This book is to pass on the legacy of who she was, and to illustrate that everyone can enjoy the passion, love, and personal relationship with God by intentionally doing so, as she so obviously did.

I believe, as my nephew, Tim Fraumann, said, "God took Aunt Jan to heaven because He has a bigger assignment for her in heaven than here on earth." And as my dear friend Reverend Rory Wineka shared with me, Revelation 14:13, "And I heard a voice in heaven saying unto me, write, blessed are the dead which die in the Lord from henceforth: yea, sayeth the Spirit, that they may rest from their labors; and their works do follow them."

This book is my attempt for Jan's life, inspiration, ministry, and works to follow her and be her legacy. Her main passion was being good wife and mother.

Praise the Lord, what a ministry, what a legacy!!!

Her Loving Husband,

Robert "Bob" Fraumann

QR

This book contains many QR's.

- A QR Code is a "Quick Response" Code.

- It is a mobile phone readable bar code.

- If you have the QR reader app on your smartphone, it will automatically link you to that video on YouTube.

- You can then follow along with the text of the specific chapter in this book.

- There are ten QR's throughout these chapters.

- If you do not have the QR reader app currently on your smartphone, you can search for it online and download this app for free.

- Otherwise, use the URL web address beside the QR Code to access the YouTube videos in this book.

Here is Jan singing on YouTube
with a PowerPoint of her life.

http://tinyurl.com/JanSinging

About the Author

Robert (Bob) Frederick Fraumann I, was born and raised in Pittsburgh, PA, and worshipped at the Christian and Missionary Alliance Church.

Bob attended Asbury (College) University in Wilmore, KY (1954-1958) and earned his Bachelor of Arts (AB) degree in Music Education, with a major in Organ Performance and a minor in Voice and Conducting.

While Bob was a student at Asbury, he traveled over forty thousand miles in a Gospel Team, "Youth Crusaders," with George Morris, Robert Carpenter, and Jerry Dooling, for two and one-half years conducting over fifty revivals in twenty-four states and witnessed over six hundred and fifty young people make decisions for Christ in their lives. Unbelievably, all four young men were still only teenagers.

During this time in college, he met Janice (Jan) Marie Brown. They dated, became engaged, and married in 1957. He also served three student Methodist churches during his college days:

- First Methodist Church, Wilmore, KY
- Centenary Methodist Church, Lexington, KY
- First Methodist Church, Harrodsburg, KY

Bob then attended Westminster Choir College in Princeton, NJ (1958-1960) for graduate work, where he earned his Master's Degree (M.M.) in Music with a major in Conducting and a minor in Organ and Voice. He sang many times in Carnegie Hall with Leonard Bernstein and other conductors with the New York Philharmonic Orchestra, singing major choral works including Beethoven's Ninth Symphony.

While in New Jersey, he served two Presbyterian churches:
- First Presbyterian Church, Woodbridge, NJ
- First Presbyterian Church, Avenel, NJ

From 1960-present, Bob has served four Methodist churches in Kentucky and Georgia (fifty-four years) as Minister of Music, Organist, and directing a graded choir program from age four through adult:
- Centenary United Methodist Church, Ashland, KY
- First United Methodist Church, East Point, GA
- First United Methodist Church, Sandy Springs, GA
- Mt. Zion United Methodist Church, Marietta, GA

He has toured with his youth choirs around the United States and Jamaica for over fifty years, performing in over a thousand concerts. Bob has privately taught piano, organ, trumpet, and voice to thousands of students. He has ministered together with over forty pastors in the past sixty years.

He and his wife, Jan, traveled extensively as music clinicians and motivational speakers throughout the United States, Jamaica, and the Caribbean.

In 2010, Senator Johnny Isakson of Georgia invited Bob to play piano at the National Prayer Breakfast in Washington, D.C. Also, Bob and his Chancel Choir at Mt. Zion United Methodist Church, Marietta, Georgia, sang with Stephen Curtis Chapman at Carnegie Hall in New York City in 2014.

Bob and Jan were happily married for fifty-six years. They have two sons, Rick and Greg, who each married wonderful Christian women, which led to four grandchildren, and three great-grandchildren.

Bob produced a CD of piano music, which is a blend of classical and Christian music, and a joke book of over four hundred jokes, which can be found at www.bobfraumann.com.

Janice Fraumann

http://bobfraumann.com/

These were the revival posters we used for two and a half years while traveling through twenty-four states from North Dakota and New Mexico and all points east.

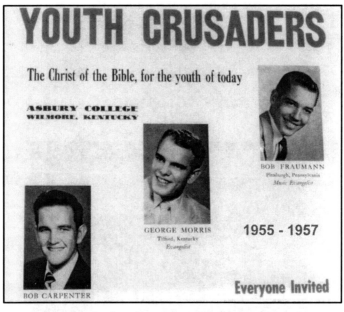

Dedication

This book is dedicated with much love, thanks, and appreciation to:

GOD: Who made all this possible to me. I thank you, God, for leading me to Jan, the second most important decision I made in my life, after accepting YOU in my life at age twelve, and then to marry Jan. She supported me one hundred percent in every endeavor and decision I made including:

- My church music ministry
- Real estate investments
- Wedding catering
- Credit business
- Importing
- Motivational speaking
- Private teaching
- Marketing and management

RICK & GREG: Our two sons, who were privileged to be raised by a saint and now carry on her legacy.

MAMA MAE: Jan's mother, Julia Mae Curry Brown, with love and thanks for especially taking extremely good care of Jan for a year in her healing from polio at age twelve. This required daily care with physical therapy and "praise God," He healed Jan, when the doctors said it was impossible. Mama Mae passed away at ninety-five on February 8, 2014, almost six months after Jan.

**My dear wife, Jan
(August 7, 1938 – August 12, 2013)
WOW! What a lady, wife, mother, supporter, and saint.**

Appreciation

Transcribing
Tani Gilliam ....Friend
Rick Fraumann ....Son
Greg Fraumann ....Son

Artwork
Roberta Grimme... Friend

Photography
Rick Rice.. Friend
Don and Debbie Evans ....Friend
Rebecca Ruscitti ....Friend

Video Recordings and YouTube
Ken Grimme... Friend

Proofreaders
Dr. Hugh and Betty Sue Cauthen ....Former Pastor and Wife
Jorja Davis ....Friend
Dan and Becca Farr .... Friends
Beth Janes ....Occupational Therapist
The Rev. Jerry Meredith ....Friend
Dr. George Morris............College friend, Pastor, and Professor
Donna Rice ....Friend

Technical Advisors
Brett Decker ....Friend
Ken Grimme... Friend

Counsel & Encouragement
Dr. Hugh and Betty Sue Cauthen ....Former Pastor and Wife
Dan and Becca Farr .... Friends
Dan and Lynn Hummer .... Friends
The Rev. Tom Pilgrim .... Former Pastor

Editors
Dan and Becca Farr...................................... Friends
Jorja Davis ....Friend

Chapter One

Article from Columbus, Georgia Newspaper

'New' Legs for Easter

12-Year-Old Wins Over Polio to
Join in Sunday's Parade

Janice will don her new dress and hat tomorrow morning and join the Easter Parade, strolling happily to church, like thousands of other twelve-year-old girls over the nation.

But Easter this year will have an added meaning for Janice Brown, who was stricken six months ago with crippling poliomyelitis. Tomorrow, she will walk – alone and without any cane or crutches – outside her home for the first time since her affliction.

"In a sense, I'm having my own little private 'resurrection,'" laughed the young, lovely daughter of Mr. and Mrs. J.B. Brown, as she tried on her Easter "outfit" today in preparation of tomorrow's extra-special occasion.

Author's note: The vaccine for poliomyelitis was not invented until 1961, which was at least ten years after Jan's miracle.

Jan in "polio bed" isolation at age 12.

Easter Sunday age 13.

Chapter Two
Jan's Personal Testimony

What a joy it is to have a love relationship with God.

It all began many years ago when I was a young girl.

At the age of twelve, I was struck with the dreaded disease of that time period . . . polio, with no cure.

I was put in the hospital . . . in isolation. My parents were the only ones who could visit me, and they had to wear masks, gowns, and gloves when they came in the room. I was lonely and afraid.

One night as my parents were leaving my room, the doctor stopped them right outside my door. I could hear them talking.

I heard the prognosis.

The doctor told my parents that:

I would never walk again
I would never be able to have children
I would never live an ordinary, normal life

My parents asked a few questions, and then they all left. I had overheard something I was not supposed to hear.

I was alone . . . and afraid. . . and it was dark!!!
I prayed.

Yes, I knew how to pray. I had godly grandparents who prayed every time I visited them. They prayed at meal time and they prayed before they went to bed.

During those nighttime prayers, Papa Lee would always pray for each of his CHILDREN and all us GRANDCHILDREN by name. It was nice . . . it was reassuring to hear him pray for ME, to call my name in prayer.

So, I prayed in that hospital room. I was afraid and I told God I wanted a relationship with Him. I wanted Him to be real in my life.

I promised Him I would live for Him and give my entire life to Him. I asked if He would be merciful to me and heal me and let me live an ordinary, normal life.

God's healing was not instantaneous. It took about a month in the hospital, and a year of being bedridden before I walked again at the age of thirteen.

I then was homeschooled for a year and progressed as fast as I learned. I completed grades ten through twelve in one year and graduated from high school at age fifteen. At age sixteen, God led me to a Christian college, Asbury (College) University, in Wilmore, KY. I met Bob Fraumann there.

I had asked God for a Christian husband. I had already listed the qualifications for my knight in shining armor. (See the chapter entitled Thirty Qualities for Dating).

When I met Bob, he was everything I had hoped for . . . and more.

We dated and fell in love. I fell head over heels in love with him . . . and I still am.

He has been the spiritual leader in our home. Bob's faith has been like a rock.

When I need someone to pray for me, I ask my husband. I know God hears his prayers.

James 5:16b, "The prayer of a righteous man is powerful and effective."

What a time we have had! The weekend after our honeymoon, Bob started working as youth and music director in Centenary Methodist Church, Lexington, KY. Next, he served First Methodist Church, Harrodsburg, KY, as Organist, Choir Director, and Youth Director. After graduation, he went to Westminster Choir College, Princeton, NJ, for graduate work and his Master's Degree (M.M.) I taught fifth grade at age nineteen. He's been working for God in churches ever since.

Bob has taken youth choir tours every summer for over fifty years. He has been Minister of Music, Choir Director, Organist, Youth Director . . . one or more positions ever since we married, and I have had the privilege of being included.

It is so exciting to experience God in your life.

Oh, young people, it is the best decision you can make. The decision to have a love relationship with God and to be obedient and work where he is working.

Back to me and my prayer in the hospital, in summary.

- Yes, I did walk again . . . and I've kept walking.
- Yes, I did have children, two wonderful sons.
- Yes, I have NOT had an ordinary life . . . but an extraordinary life with God as my friend and guide.

This love relationship I have had with God is what makes life so special!

Thank you, God!!!

5

Chapter Three
My Tribute to God

http://tinyurl.com/JanFraumann

Jan Fraumann
January 2013

Guest Speaker, United Methodist Women Sunday

Mt. Zion United Methodist Church Marietta, GA

I was born in Columbus, GA. I'm a southern lady. When I was twelve years old, polio struck Columbus and polio struck me. And so I was put in the hospital in isolation. It affected my left leg, my back and my whole left side.

I was in the hospital in isolation. My parents were my only visitors. They would come in white gowns and white masks and have to leave them before they left. One night they left my room and I heard them in the hall talking to the doctor. I could hear them, but they didn't know I could. And the doctor said I want to talk to y'all about your daughter. She'll never walk again. She'll never have children. And she'll never live a normal life. And I thought, "that can't be me…I'm just twelve, I'm a child, I have my whole life ahead of me. What do I do?!" And I was there alone. (sigh)… I prayed. I knew how to pray, because I had a Mama Julia and a Papa Lee. Papa Lee was a preacher and every time we went to their house, before we left, he made us get in the living room in a circle and he prayed for each one of us by name. Mama Julia taught me by her rocking chair the Word, and how important it was and she told me God could take me through anything.

She was a widow with three children and God took her through, provided for her. She told me God would give me the desires of my heart. And no matter what happened in life, I should turn to Him and He would take care of me. So I prayed, because I knew how. I had it modeled before me. Not necessarily my parents....my grandparents, and my uncle and aunt who were very godly.

I asked God, "Please God, help me walk again, and help me have children and a wonderful husband, and help me have a normal life". And you know, He answered all of those prayers. In less than a year, I was walking again. They had an article in the paper "New Legs for Easter" and my picture. It was a miracle! It really was! So I know there are miracles and there are answers to prayer.

After that, I went to a private school and took tenth, eleventh & twelfth grades in one year and graduated from high school at age fifteen. I went to Asbury (College) University at age sixteen. And the first year I was there, I remember writing a letter to God and putting it in my Bible...the kind of husband I wanted. I knew a lot of things I didn't want and I asked God to help me write a list of what I did want. Of course, I wanted tall and good-looking, you know. That had to be in there. But I wanted somebody that could be a spiritual leader in my family. I wanted him to be my spiritual leader. I wanted him to be a strong man of faith; a godly man who loves the Lord and wanted to serve Him.

And I would pray over that list and I would put it back in my Bible. And it wasn't long until I met Bob and dated him and I'd go home and look at the list. And he was just everything on the list and more. Well, we fell in love and we married while we were still in college. I was eighteen and he was twenty. I wasn't going to let him get away. The last year in college we were married and the next year we went to New Jersey and I was teaching school when I was nineteen. I was teaching fifth grade. And Bob was getting his Master's Degree at Westminster Choir College in Princeton, New Jersey.

Now, I want to tell y'all…I'll try not to cry. But the greatest treasure God has given me…is Bob. He has been the most wonderful husband. We have been married fifty-five years. He's my best friend. In my down times, he is there. In my happy times, he's there. I can wake him up in the night and say "Bob, please pray for me. I need your prayers". And he will. He's been a wonderful man of God; a spiritual leader for our family. And he's been a wonderful choir director. And just a wonderful man and I thank God for that treasure.

My life goals were to be a good wife and mother. My mother kept saying "Why do you do this, you're happy?" And I said, "Well, I need to learn, Mother." I didn't have everything patterned in front of me so I need to learn. So, I studied every book I could and went to every class I could on how to be a better wife or mother. I've made a lot of mistakes. I'd like to go back and correct some of them, but we don't get that option. But, I do think it was my heart's desire to be that. And it still is.

We raised two sons, Rick and Greg. Both asked Jesus into their hearts at home. And Bob and I got to pray with them and lead them to the Lord. Both boys married girls who love the Lord. Laura and Terri are amazing wives and mothers. I love them; I don't have daughters, so they are my daughters. And they love our sons. And they are good to them and they make a wonderful Christian home for our grandchildren and our sons.

Now before our children were born, I prayed for them and I prayed for my grandchildren too…the same way. I prayed that they would be healthy and normal. And I prayed they'd be good-lookin'. And I prayed that they would have a tender heart toward the Lord, so if they strayed, I felt like the Lord could call them back. And I prayed for their wives…before they were born. I prayed that they would find the right wife for them that would be a godly woman.

Well, in 2003, our boys had moved away. I never thought they'd leave Atlanta. Rick moved to Texas for a job. Greg moved to Ohio for a wife. And so they were both living far away in 2003 when I went to the doctor with a lump in my right thigh, upper thigh. And, they sent me to another doctor, and another doctor. I went through three or four doctors and a lot of testing. During that time, one of the doctors mentioned sarcoma and malignancy and it frightened me to pieces.

At 4:00 A.M. every morning, that fear would enter my bedroom. It wouldn't wake Bob, but it would wake me. A spirit of fear I call it, because that's what the Bible calls it. The Bible says, "God has not given us the spirit of fear, but of love and power and a sound mind." But that fear would come like a black cloud, all over that room, and I could hardly breathe. It would take my breath away. I don't know, it was fear of cancer, it was fear of dying. It was just fear. And I prayed and I read the Bible and I quoted that scripture about fear. But it didn't go away. They were still doing tests and I said we want to go see our son in Texas, and they said, well go, and come back we will have your test results then. We went out there and Rick said, "Mom, we're going to pray for you tonight." So, they put me in the lounge chair and Rick got at my head and anointed me with oil. And Bob was at one side and Laura at the other and Bobby and Brittany were at my feet. And they each one prayed for me and went around. And Rick rebuked that spirit of fear. I believe it's a spirit and I don't believe it's a good spirit.

He rebuked that spirit of fear and said, "Leave my mother. I rebuke you in the name of Jesus and don't you ever come back and bother my mother. You go in the name of Jesus and in Jesus' blood."

I want you to know…that fear left! It left! The most wonderful thing!

Now, it's tried to come back and I try to imitate what Rick did and I rebuke that spirit and it goes.

I had radiation surgery pretty deep in the leg. I had to learn to walk again. I learned to walk right here in this aisle holding one pew to the

9

next and praying to my good shepherd up behind me.

The original sarcoma never came back. What came back was radiation induced tumors. I didn't know radiation could do that, but it can and it did. I've had seven surgeries since then on my right leg and during that time they tested a breast and thought I had a tumor below the breast, it was pre-cancer, so they did an operation for breast cancer.

During those times, I searched the Scriptures.

"I will be with you always, even unto the end of the age."
"I am thy God who heals you."
"By your stripes I am healed."
"I can do all things through Christ who strengthens me."

I wrote many, many scriptures (Chapter Four) ... every scripture I could find on healing. I wrote and I read and I prayed and I believed. And I prayed for faith and more faith.

Well, it was nine years until last year...last January the 10th, 2012. I was standing in our kitchen. We had visited our son in Ohio and we had gone through the Amish country and we'd come back with a load of apples. We were standing in the kitchen and Bob and I were both peeling apples and I stood and twisted my leg, twisted my foot and I guess pivoted and I heard a snap and excruciating pain. My walker was there with a seat so Bob came over and had me sit down – helped me sit in the chair and called 911.

I thank God my doctor was here that had done all the surgeries. I wasn't in another state. I thank God that all that was worked out. When I went to the hospital they did tests and on the 13th they came in early and said we can't save the leg, Jan. It's broken and the bone is compromised from the radiation and a plate won't hold it. So the only option we have is amputation.

Well, I had to decide by noon and he was going to get the operating room ready at 2:00 P.M. Well, by the time I got to the operating room and was in there, there was a host of Mt. Zion people in the waiting room with Bob to pray with him and stay with him and pray with me. I thank you Mt. Zion.

So I went in and had the amputation. The boys came in different weeks and that was a great help to see them. I was sent to Manor Care and then had to come back for another operation because of the infection. I was in Manor Care for ninety days. They were wonderful to me in every way. It was wonderful rehab. But I tell people I've been to hell and back. And it happened at Manor Care. Every night, satan would come in and talk to me. I would sleep with all the lights on.

And one night when I was in such pain, and there were times I was on so many drugs, I did not even know anybody. I couldn't converse. But anyway, it was when I was getting a little better and he would come and tell me that God did not love me. "Who do you know Jan, that is an amputee? You don't know anybody like you. You'll never have a life." And I said, "satan, I prayed that if God wanted to take me, I was ready when they operated. But He's left me here, so evidently it's for some reason." And so, he kept on and said, "You will never have a life, you won't get to see your grandchildren. You'll be in bed the rest of your life." And I listened and I listened. And one night I just got tired of it. And I said, "satan, you are nothing but a liar. You are the father of lies. You want to lie, you want to kill, you want to destroy. You want to do that to me and to all God's children. And I tell you what, I rebuke you," and I did like Rick...I rebuked him in the name of Jesus and Jesus' blood and said, "Get out of here and don't come back. Go wherever God sends you, but you're not welcome here and I'm not gonna listen to you...anymore."

And then I asked God to give me the strength to be positive. And I made a decision that I was going to take what I had and see what was left. And if I could make a life out of what was left of me.

And so, I decided to read and to study and to be positive and look for blessings and look for good. Three blessings a day I've been looking

11

for ever since then. And I write them down at night. So I get up every morning looking at God's blessings and they're always there.

I want to tell you this is a wonderful church family; you will not find a better one in all the world. You've been so good to us. The choir, the Bible studies, the ministers, the meals you've sent. Hundreds of meals, the hundreds of prayers, the hundreds of cards...I have every one of them. You know how you know Christians? Is it because they come to church and say they're born again? No...you'll know them by their love. And I can tell you there are some wonderful loving Christians in this church and I am proud of you and I love you and I thank you.

I want to challenge families to teach prayer by example. Just like I had a Mama and a Papa; maybe you're going to have to be that person in your family. One hour of church weekly is not enough. When people come to me and say, I just don't get enough out of church, I say, "I know what you mean, I feel the same way. I don't get enough. A twenty minute sermon is not enough for me; I wish the preachers would preach an hour!" That's why I decided to join Bible studies because I could satisfy that desire for more and more of God and more and more of His Word.

Our children and grandchildren pray for us. I never thought of them praying for us. We prayed for them all their lives. They'll get on the phone and they'll pray for us. I want to tell you to never give up on your children. Never give up on their relationship with God. Never give up on your family. I prayed for my brother for over forty-five years and before he died he found the Lord in a great, marvelous way. So, pray that your children will have that love relationship with God; that personal relationship.

Rick and Greg are grown now. I don't know where the time flew. But they're grown and they are godly men. I want to tell you two stories about their growing up. One was, this was before cell phones, so they each had a line in their bedrooms; a private line for their counseling service because in high school, they were counseling kids all the time.

Kids would come to the house or they would call and have problems and our children would pray with them and tell them about Jesus.

Another thing is I raised our children that Fraumanns are different. We're not like everybody else. When you tell me that everybody is doing it or everybody is going…that doesn't mean that it's us. So we're different. We're like fish with a backbone. We can swim upstream. Fish without a backbone just go downstream with all the muck and all the dirt and all the fish. We have a choice. We have a backbone. We have a choice and we can stand up for our beliefs and we don't mind being different because we are Christians.

Both of our sons married godly girls. They have godly homes. You can feel the Holy Spirit in their homes. And I love Laura and Terri. Since not having girls, they're my girls and I love and appreciate them so much.

Rick and Laura, Rick is our older one in Texas, have two children. Bobby is our only grandson. Sabrina he married. Sabrina loves the Lord. She's a prayer warrior and she's a ballet dancer. And Bobby is a Marine. You know once a Marine, always a Marine. And he's a Youth Director in his church and he's on the praise team and he is sold out to the Lord. All he wants to talk about is the Lord and the Bible and God's grace. And it's just so wonderful. Bobby and Sabrina gave us our first and second great-grandchildren. Cadence is two and Michaela, a girl, is nine months old.

Rick and Laura have a daughter, Brittany. Some of you remember she danced here. She married a young man named Nate, who is a Marine also. He loves the Word; he's a student of the Word. He and Bobby study the Word together a lot.

Brittany is our oldest granddaughter and is a dancer also. She has her own dance studio, *Dance to Glory*, where she teaches little girls to dance and love Jesus. Brittany is a prayer warrior. She's a wonderful cook. Wonderful birthday cakes she makes. Brittany and Nate gave us our third great-grandchild, Johnathan Robert. He was born when we were out there this Christmas. He was born January 2nd, this month. And we got to hold him when he was only one hour old. How wonderful!

Greg and Terri, Greg's our younger son in Ohio. Greg and Terri have two girls, Victoria is twelve and Sofia is seven; Terri homeschools now. Laura homeschooled her children from kindergarten through high school, and now Terri is homeschooling their children in Ohio.

Victoria and Sofia love to dance. They love ballet and are taking three or four different kinds of dance. They belong to a wonderful church who teaches the Word. Victoria loves the Lord. She has her own prayer journal at twelve and loves writing scriptures in her journal. Sofia is seven and she loves Jesus and when she was three, she would get on the phone and she would say, "Dear heavenly Father, I pray that Mama Jan would get well so she can come see me." And she still prays with me over the phone, both of them do.

TO GOD BE THE GLORY. I'm not telling you any of this because Bob and I are not special. God has blessed us in so many ways. Yes, we've had heartaches; we've had trials. I have been at the bottom, but I still can praise God for what he has done. I praise him for our family. Mama Mae, my mother, is ninety-four and still living. She is a great-great-grandmother and she lives with her granddaughter in Newnan, GA, Julie and Stephen and their children Catelin and Brandon. And they are so good to my mother, they are so good to Mama Mae and Mama Mae is very happy.

Sometimes we think we are in control of our lives. In one split second everything can change forever. Happiness is based on our circumstances, but joy comes from the Lord. So, I have prayed for joy and I have prayed for peace and I continue to pray for them. God is helping me live life. When they took the leg, they took all the cancer in that leg with it, so praise be to God.

We took a family vacation in June. We flew to Rick's in Texas in August. We flew to Greg's in Ohio for Thanksgiving and we flew to

Rick's in Texas over Christmas. So, God is helping me live and the devil lied. See, he's just a liar.

And I can tell you if you have nothing but God, He's enough. He is enough! I have proved it! I have proved it! And He loves you. And there were times that I prayed and He didn't hear me. He wasn't there. I couldn't understand. Then, there were times when the Holy Spirit would sweep over me and He was so close. Oh, I love those times. But, I want you to know He is there…working in the background sometimes when you don't even know it.

If you would like prayer after the service, I am going to ask you just to come up here and pray with me. I'll pray with you and the ministers are at the altar. If you have sickness or disease and you want to pray. If somebody in your family does. If you are burdened for somebody, about their lifestyle, if you're burdened because somebody is not born again or saved in your family, if you're burdened for finances for somebody, a friend you need to pray for, I'm going to ask you just to come up and we're going to pray together after the service.

I taught a blessing class one time here not too long ago and I may do another one if God allows, where you bless your children and you bless your grandchildren and teach you how to do that. And so this is this Priestly Blessing that is in the Bible. God gave Moses this blessing to end the services in the temple, and he told Aaron to do it. And this is the Priestly Blessing…

"The Lord bless you and keep you.
The Lord make His face to shine upon you and be gracious to you.
The Lord lift His countenance upon you and give you peace.
Amen."

Chapter Four
Healing Scriptures

Jan loved to read healing scriptures daily. She felt that these positive scriptures were like medicine to her soul and body to bring her healing. Following are just a few examples of these beautiful scriptures with promise:

OLD TESTAMENT

Exodus 23:25 (KJV)
And ye shall serve the LORD your God, and he shall bless thy bread, and thy water; and I will take sickness away from the midst of thee.

Psalm 30:2 (KJV)
O LORD my God, I cried unto thee, and thou hast healed me.

Psalm 103:1-3 (KJV)
Bless the LORD, O my soul: and all that is within me, bless his holy name.
Bless the LORD, O my soul, and forget not all his benefits:
Who forgiveth all thine iniquities; who healeth all thy diseases.

Psalm 107:20 (KJV)
He sent his Word, and healed them, and delivered them from their destructions.

Proverbs 3:5-8 (KJV)
Trust in the LORD with all thine heart; and lean not unto thine own understanding. In all thy ways acknowledge him, and he shall direct thy paths. Be not wise in thine own eyes: fear the LORD, and depart from evil. It shall be health to thy navel, and marrow to thy bones.

16

Isaiah 53:5 (KJV)
But he was wounded for our transgressions; he was bruised for our iniquities: the chastisement of our peace was upon him; and with his stripes we are healed.

Jeremiah 30:17a (KJV)
For I will restore health unto thee, and I will heal thee of thy wounds, saith the LORD

NEW TESTAMENT

Matthew 4:23 (KJV)
And Jesus went about all Galilee, teaching in their synagogues, and preaching the gospel of the kingdom, and healing all manner of sickness and all manner of disease among the people.

Matthew 8:2-3 (KJV)
And, behold, there came a leper and worshipped him, saying, Lord, if thou wilt, thou canst make me clean. And Jesus put forth his hand, and touched him, saying, I will; be thou clean. And immediately his leprosy was cleansed.

Matthew 9:29 (KJV)
Then touched he their eyes, saying, According to your faith be it unto you.

Matthew 14:35-36 (KJV)
And when the men of that place had knowledge of him, they sent out into all that country round about, and brought unto him all that were diseased; And besought him that they might only touch the hem of his garment: and as many as touched were made perfectly whole.

Matthew 15:30 (KJV)
And great multitudes came unto him, having with them those that were lame, blind, dumb, maimed, and many others, and cast them down at Jesus' feet; and he healed them.

Matthew 21:22 (KJV)
And all things, whatsoever ye shall ask in prayer, believing, ye shall receive.

Mark 10:27 (KJV)
And Jesus looking upon them saith, with men it is impossible, but not with God: for with God all things are possible.

Mark 11:22-24 (KJV)
And Jesus answering saith unto them, Have faith in God. For verily I say unto you, That whosoever shall say unto this mountain, be thou removed, and be thou cast into the sea; and shall not doubt in his heart, but shall believe that those things which he saith shall come to pass; he shall have whatsoever he saith. Therefore I say unto you, what things soever ye desire, when ye pray, believe that ye receive them, and ye shall have them.

Luke 4:40 (KJV)
Now when the sun was setting, all they that had any sick with divers diseases brought them unto him; and he laid his hands on every one of them, and healed them.

Luke 11:9-10 (KJV)
And I say unto you, ask, and it shall be given you; seek, and ye shall find; knock, and it shall be opened unto you. For every one that asketh receiveth; and he that seeketh findeth; and to him that knocketh it shall be opened.

Luke 17:12-14 (KJV)
And as he entered into a certain village, there met him ten men that were lepers, which stood afar off: And they lifted up their voices, and said, Jesus, Master, have mercy on us. And when he saw them, he said unto them, Go shew yourselves unto the priests. And it came to pass, that, as they went, they were cleansed.

Acts 9:32-34 (KJV)
And it came to pass, as Peter passed throughout all quarters, he came down also to the saints which dwelt at Lydda. And there he found a certain man named Aeneas, which had kept his bed eight years, and was sick of the palsy. And Peter said unto him, Aeneas, Jesus Christ maketh thee whole: arise, and make thy bed. And he arose immediately.

Philippians 4:6 (KJV)
Be careful for nothing; but in every thing by prayer and supplication with thanksgiving let your requests be made known unto God.

James 5:14-15a (KJV)
Is any sick among you? Let him call for the elders of the church; and let them pray over him, anointing him with oil in the name of the Lord: And the prayer of faith shall save the sick, and the Lord shall raise him up.

First Peter 2:24 (KJV)
Who his own self bare our sins in his own body on the tree, that we, being dead to sins, should live unto righteousness: by whose stripes ye were healed.

Third John 1:2 (KJV)
Beloved, I wish above all things that thou mayest prosper and be in health, even as thy soul prospereth.

Chapter Five
Conversations with God

Jan had personal conversations with God and journaled them over a sixteen year period from 1991-2007. I discovered over three hundred pages of these conversations after her death. I knew she kept a journal, and I knew it was very private. Following are excerpts of these very exciting conversations.

A Note From The Editor:

"I cannot tell you how powerful this section was. I read these conversations about halfway through, put the book down, and rested with great peace for about an hour."
Dan Farr

February 10, 1991

HOLY SPIRIT: I want you to keep a journal. If you keep it all together, it will serve to remind you of My promises and My promises fulfilled.

I have promised you much in the past and I will continue to promise you much in the future.

You want to live a life with calmness and peace. This will help.

Now, let's take things step by step.

It's true, you cannot change the past, but you can let go of the past. Cut the cords that bind you and keep you looking back. No matter how sad or happy the past was, it is gone – and gone forever. Start today with Me. Feel My presence in and around you.

Allow Me to submerge you with My Spirit. I can heal all the hurts, the pains and restore unto you all that was lost plus increase it 7x7.

You are My child. I have not left you. Have I not taken care of you? You are treated like a queen by your husband. I gave Bob to you. It has been his joy to take care of you, not his burden.

I am in charge. Have I not done a good job so far? Keep turning things over to Me – and be FREE.

If you could feel the freedom and abandon that's possible by living in My Spirit, you would be free to pursue. You could set goals and attain them.

You could give of yourself again and not worry about the consequences.

I want you to be happy. You can't be happy and worry. I want to help you quit worrying. It is too stressful. It takes too much JOY away.

Bob wants you to be joyful, happy, laughing. So do I. Let Go – and let God.

Now, I don't have to tell you to hold onto things, to manage or keep things under control. You do that. What I say is, "Lighten Up." Give Me complete control. Allow yourself to have creative ideas that flow, not stopped by negative thinking or meanderings.

You are in a wonderful time of your life. I want you to enjoy it.

March 3, 1991

JAN: What a joy to wake up, and you're here.

HOLY SPIRIT: I've got some things I want to tell you today.

You are strong in Me. Whatever happens, you can depend on Me. Life is not always easy. Find your solace in Me. I'll never leave you nor forsake you.

Please don't think for one minute My power is limited to yours. I have unlimited power. Ask – I will show you great and wondrous things.

I am in control of every part of your life and every decision. I hold you in the palm of My hand. You are there now. Never fear. My eyes and thoughts never forsake you. You are My own. You were bought with a price. You are My treasure. I will always be with you. I will never leave you nor forsake you.

July 6, 1991

HOLY SPIRIT: Do you believe I am in charge of things?

JAN: Yes, however, I need Your assurance.

HOLY SPIRIT: O.K.

Put everything in a category, pray over it, and allow Me to work it out. Some things take time. I have not lost control or forgotten you. You still want the whole plan rather than the daily adventure.

The daily adventure is the thrill of it all. The closeness to Me, knowing I am there. Liken it to a child growing up – you want to be an adult – to get there. Enjoy each day, as a child does. Do not worry or fret about the future. Enjoy each hour, each task, each experience. Slow down and live.

Look to Me as your source.

Am I in control or not?
Either I am – or I am not.
If I'm not, you have every reason to fret and worry.
If I am – you need have no fear. Then you are free to enjoy life. Live life with abandonment. Your life is not your own. Your life is being designed by the Great Designer.

Allow Me to move freely in your life. Allow Me to bring the right people to you. Allow Me flexibility. Don't be so rigid.

Plan your calendar, but live one day at a time. Today is enough to carry. Enjoy today's blessings and challenges. Live today passionately.

Allow Me to touch you and bless you.

Write your list of things you need and I will bless them. Bring all your cares and troubles to Me. I hear your every Word, every complaint. I know your mind and heart. Bring it all to Me – and then rest.

February 23, 1992

JAN: It is 3:00 A.M. and I'm not asleep. I was so upset tonight. Things are "grabbing" me and I feel as though evil spirits are trying to pull at me.

HOLY SPIRIT: Turn it all over to Me, Jan. I have never left you – oh, you may think I have, but I haven't.

Now – look around you. You love your house, the way it's decorated. You are happy here.

If we are going to tackle things together, you are going to have to trust Me. I can only lead when you follow. You must learn to listen to My voice.

Now – I'm speaking to you.

You are My sheep; you know the sound of My voice – the Shepherd's voice.

Fear is not of Me. Cast out all fear. I have not called you to fear. I have called you to follow.

I am in charge.

Do what your hands find to do – do what you know to do and leave the rest to Me.

Bob – He is My man. I will uphold him. I will hold him in the hollow of My hand. He is faithful to Me, I will be faithful to him. I will give him long life – yes, vibrant health.

Think of what can be, not what is now. I will heal all your diseases. You are mine.

Your worry and fretting are making you sick. You must STOP IT NOW!

Don't worry about your children one minute. I am with them. They know My voice as well or better than yours.

Peace I give you; not as the world giveth. Let not your heart be troubled. Ye believe in God – believe also in Me.

Honey - you are Mine. I have bought you with a great price. In My Father's house are many mansions. I go there to prepare a place for you, that where I am, there you may be also. But until then, listen to Me.

I am taking care of your children, right? You have anything and almost everything you want, right? Then, you are upset – not about your needs – but about your wants, right? And your wants are concerned with your security, right? You are trying to plan your security, right? Let ME do it for you. You follow ME.

You walk in the light I give. If there is no light, don't walk. I will show you the path and make it plain. I will light your way. Do you think it pleases Me to see you at 3:00 a.m. – anxious? No – My Word says – Be anxious for nothing, but in everything, by prayer and supplication, and thanksgiving let your requests be made known unto Me. And – the peace of God which passeth all understanding shall keep your hearts and minds through Jesus Christ our Lord.

Now – you have prayed in supplication – with thanksgiving – do THAT – and My peace will come. Start thanking Me for what I have done, am doing, and will do. The peace will come. My peace will come. Then the joy of righteous living will be yours. You deserve joy, happiness, and peace – only I can give it. I give it to you, Jan, because you ask, you seek – you shall find. Let go – and let Me have a chance! I love you.

October 3, 1992

HOLY SPIRIT: Dear One, be still and know that I am God. My sheep KNOW My voice. You've heard My voice all your life. Why are you doubting now?

JAN: Please speak to me Lord. I love and praise You. None other is so great in all the world. You have been with me all my life. You have surrounded me with those who loved me unconditionally.

I am most blessed by You. You gave Bob to me – my greatest treasure. You gave my sons to me – my greatest joy. You have given grandchildren to me.

HOLY SPIRIT: Jan, listen closely, I'm going to speak. Take up your bed and walk. I heal your body. Take up your cross and go to work. I will make a way – a clear path for you in the wilderness. I will never leave you or forsake you. I am with you always, even unto the end of the world.

Hold on with all your might. Do not listen to the voices of another. They would lead you astray. Keep calm and listen to My voice daily. I have it all worked out. My greatest wish is that you could be joyous during this period. I want your happiness and I want you to be joyous. Do not fret. Do not be anxious. Do not get confused – you know who the author of confusion is.

Your boat is not going to sink. Look beyond the waves. Believe in clear skies – and clear sailing ahead. Believe it. Put your faith in it.

Today I will show you many great and wonderful things. Believe and trust Me – you have all your life. Just trust Me for wealth, health, happiness and trust Me for eternity.
Your life should be ALL JOY. What do you possibly have to gripe or complain about? Count it all joy – and go on.

Keep on keeping on.

God is the pilot of your little boat – or your big ship. You don't know how to pilot it, but God does. Rely on Him. If He is the pilot, all the responsibility rests on Him. You are free to be a joyful passenger. Have fun. Love life.

Don't be in such a rush. You act as though you're in a hurry to meet

Me – know that I am with you every step of the way. Slow down and know that I walk with you. You don't have to rush to meet Me. I am here.

Thoughts about satan! Learn his ways. Because you chose to ignore him – he deceived you. Learn the evil one's ways. Don't be numb to satan. Be wise.

I expect you to TRUST ME, BELIEVE ME, RELY on ME. Be happy and know I AM in control, I AM! You are not! Now, if you want My blessings, pray and thank Me more. I do not respond to whining.

You seem to take time for everyone but Me. I am a jealous God. I need you to spend time with Me. You can listen to TV, tapes, programs. Spend hours with Me.

The time you spend alone with Me is the most valuable time.

Relax and trust ME. I will draw all men unto you for your business. I'll guide you toward the future. I've been in the past. I'm here today. I'll be in your future. Ask Me My dreams for you. Ask Me what I want for your family. If it's what I want for you, it'll happen quickly and with no effort at all. Seek My face and I shall tell you. This week will be fine. You and I are in control. Don't try to control it yourself. Keep Me at the helm. Keep Me in charge. Keep Me charting your course. I know all the rocks and pitfalls. I can avoid the dangers you know not of. Where do you think your strength comes from? It comes from Me.

John 15:4 – "Abide in Me, and I in you." Abide together. God wants to move into your world and involve Himself totally in it – in every relationship, every business transaction, every meal, every bill, every family problem, every joy. God will be as involved with you as you'll let Him. Pray about everything. Tell God your needs and don't forget to thank Him for your answers. Philippians 4:6. "Be careful for nothing; but in everything by prayer and supplication with thanksgiving let your requests be made known unto God." 1 Peter 5:7.

"Casting all your care upon Him, for He careth for you."

Tell God your needs and don't forget to thank Him for His answers.

Why pray about everything? To open your life to God so He will be free to do whatever He wants in your life and in your circumstances.

We don't pray to get His okay on our plans. We care about circumstances. God cares about our hearts.

HOLY SPIRIT: If people don't know I am with them, they give up in despair. You must tell them I am there. I will help them.

You are the leader I choose. This is a heavy task. I said, "FEED MY SHEEP." Now is the time.

All sheep I put in your path you are to discuss with me. I will give you insight into how to help them. I will give you the energy, the health, and the fortitude to do this.

You must study again. Pray long and hard for the women and men I lead to you. Jan, they are LOST, LOST sheep. They are in a darkened world. You must shine My light. You will not be responsible for results. I will use your life and your mouth to read to My lost sheep. I am renewing you, Jan. I am renewing your spirit within you. You will be My light in a darkened world.

What I am saying to you is this – you are trying to find your purpose. I am telling you your purpose. You will be fulfilled if you know your role.

You will only be fulfilled when you walk with Me alongside of Bob. Bob is not your source. I am! He will be happier when you are happier. You will be happier when you are really close to Me and are fulfilling My desires for your life.

Pray My protection daily. Anoint your house and yourself with oil in

My name. You are ready for explosive growth. Read, take notes, write notes, send messages. I'll give you the words.

You see how people love you. Pray blessings and prosperity on them. Bless your children, your grandchildren. Have fun times when they feel your love. I will make your house a safe harbor, a retreat for those that hurt, for those that need love.

I will tell you what to do, what to say. There is so little love out there. I will pour out My love on you so you will have plenty of love for them.

What do you need that I can't provide. Make a list of your NEEDS, your WANTS, and I will give them to you.

I have chosen you, Jan, to do My work. You need a challenge – I will give you the greatest challenge of your life. But, I will be there with you. I will honor you with My presence – every time you speak, sing or talk with people. I will anoint you, my dear.

I will inspire you with ideas to do, fun to do, dreams to dream. Your last years will be your glorious years.

JAN: What is the purpose?

HOLY SPIRIT: To love the lonely, hurting, happy, confident, defeated – anyone I bring to you. Train them to be soldiers of the cross. Train them to be strong, courageous and giving, loving people in this world.

Just as bugs fly to the light, I will bring those people to you. My light will shine through you!

JAN: I don't feel worthy.

HOLY SPIRIT: You are not worthy. Worthy has nothing to do with it. I have chosen you to do My work. Haven't you been asking what

29

to do with your life? O.K. Shake off all the shackles that bind you and I will lead you.

I know you had rather love and give to children, but these adults are My children. Look at the child inside each one. Treat them with tenderness of a child, but teach them to be strong with a backbone. I will teach them the rest.

You will develop leaders around you. Of course I will do the work. You are only the vessel.

I am the Architect.
I am the Barber.
I am the Designer.
You are the vessel.

You will see what I am showing you.

Stay still. I will bring these things to you. You won't have to go out and look. I will bring it all to you. That will be My confirmation to you. My energy – not yours. My resources – not yours. My love – not yours.

April 8, 1997

HOLY SPIRIT: Read My Word. Know My ways. I will lead you in straight paths and beside still waters. You are Mine. You are bought with a price. Never worry, never fear, never look back. Look ahead, to the future. I was in the past. I am in the future.

You need to spend time with your grandchildren. They need the Fraumann talk. They are real Fraumanns.

You are in My mind's eye at all times.

August 29, 1998

HOLY SPIRIT: Today I have a few things I want to discuss with you. Putting Me first, for example. You must put Me first in your life and your activities. I know you have lots to do, but I am your Helper and I can and will help you in all that you do, if you will include Me more.

There is a difference between concern and preparation for the future and anxiety about the future. I want you to stop being anxious, but keep being concerned and prepare with My direction. Don't take a step without Me. Don't get ahead of Me, or lag too far behind. I am plotting your future. Just trust in Me. Be anxious for nothing, but in everything, by prayer and supplication, with thanksgiving, let your requests be made known unto God. And the peace of God, which passeth all understanding, shall keep your hearts and minds, through Jesus Christ, our Lord.

Now, Jan, study to show thyself approved. Study the blessing. I want you to do that today and every day until I tell you otherwise. Study the blessing. I need you to do this for Me. I need you to do it now. Don't put it off. There is an urgency! Please do this for Me! I will guide you on what to do with the information you collect.

Learn to bless your children, grandchildren, and your husband. Learn to bless Bob today. Write a blessing out for him today. Write a blessing over your home and office today. See, I want you to use the information you have, also.

Thanks for taking this early time, the first time of the day for Me. I know you love Me when you put Me first in your day. Your thoughts are of Me and I know you love Me.

I will take care of My own. You are My own. You are bought with a price . . . oh what a price I paid for you. Please don't take it lightly. Please put Me first. Then I can guide and direct your day when you ask Me to do so. I said I would order your steps. There is much to be done. Come on, dear one, and let's begin the day together. Just remember I will not leave you or forsake you . . . I will be with you all day today, and every day.

Remember, Jan, if you know ahead all of the pieces of the puzzle, then life is over. But, as in a tapestry or puzzle, you can see the picture unfolding before your eyes.

Jan, you want to know so much and be reassured so much. I want you to know and I want you to be reassured that the best is yet to come. Say that to yourself over and over. THE BEST IS YET TO COME.

Take time to be holy. Speak oft with the Lord. Look at hymns and meditate on some.

Jan, I have no shortage of water, of food, of money, of resources, of health, of blessings. Speak blessings, not curses. Think blessings, not lack. Now rejoice and be glad. I give you joy, peace, blessings, favor. Sing unto the Lord today and praise Him - - - and be GLAD - - - for He hath done marvelous works.

Spring, 1999

JAN: Thank you, Lord for the first born blessing. Thank you for giving me the gift of eternal life. Thank you, Jesus, for being willing to die on the cross for me. I can't imagine the sacrifice. God, your sacrifice of your only Son. I cannot fathom it. And, for a sinner, unworthy. And Jesus, You were willing to leave heaven to come down and suffer and die. How can I compare such love?

HOLY SPIRIT: Jan, you are doing what I want you to do. Do it daily. You can study, read, listen to the tapes, every day. You can pray and read My Word daily. I will help you out of your troubles. Just keep your mind on Me and I will keep you in perfect peace. It is the thinking about situations and trying to figure out how YOU can solve all of your problems that gets you down. Just tell Me, child, your problems. Then, go away and be happy, knowing your Father in heaven will solve all of your problems. I am the great Problem Solver. I created the universe. I own all the wealth of the world. I can solve your problems. Just turn them over to Me. Cast your care on Him, for He cares for you.

Don't be confused. You know who is the author of confusion. Just trust and obey. There is no other way to be happy in Jesus than to trust and obey. So, as you go down the road ahead, you must be happy and trust and obey. Live by faith in ME. I have promised to give you all your needs. I have promised to meet all your needs.

April 21, 1999

HOLY SPIRIT: Two years! It has been two years since I introduced you to the blessing and told you to study it.

I didn't tell you to do all the things you are doing. I told you to study the blessing.

I will teach you as we go along. You don't have time? You must take and make the time for this. This is very important to Me. You asked what I want you to do. This is it!

Now, today and every day, I want you to study the blessing. Don't get distracted. Time is precious! Time is all we have! Time is precious! Time is running out!

This is all I want you to do now. You must make and take time for this study along with all you do.

I must have your attention. I need you NOW. Others may have more time to do other things because they are not doing My work. You are accountable to ME. I expect you to start working for Me today. I cannot accept excuses. I will give you health and strength to work for Me. You must manage your time. I need your time NOW spent with Me and on My work.

June 8, 1999

HOLY SPIRIT: I will order your steps. You do not have to make it happen. When you do that, you just get frustrated. Just let Me open doors. Let Me speak to hearts. Let Me make a way where there is no way. Praise Me. Pray without ceasing.

Let us rejoice and be happy together!

Sing and be happy when your mother comes and remember the singing times when your father was alive. He enjoyed getting around the piano and singing together. Remind your family of him and his great voice.

Jan, relax and be happy. Now is the time to be happy. You are sixty, and I will cause great and wonderful things to happen in your life and in the life of your husband and children, and your children's children.

July 8, 1999

HOLY SPIRIT: Remember, Jan, an hour a day. I need an hour a day for the blessing study. Put Me first. Prioritize your life. I will help when you call on Me. Remember, "Feed My sheep." Well, this is the way I want you to feed them. I want you to bless Bob. Write out blessings now. You can certainly improve them as you go. I know the desires of your heart. I also know what you need. I promise to meet all your needs, even without your worrying and trying to fix everything. I want you to rest in Me. Rest in Me. Relax in Me. Trust Me. Have faith in Me. Believe that I love you and want the best for you.

August 15, 1999

HOLY SPIRIT: I am going to release into you My power. You will have My power. I will draw to you all you need, as you need it. I will speak through you. You are My servant, My messenger. My Spirit will be with you. Don't worry or fret. I will help you.

34

Bless Bob. Help him right now sense your spirit. Protect him. Bless him.

JAN: Lord, I need to hear from You. I love You so much and I revere Your name. You are the God of the universe. You are Holy. Your Word is truth. You are the holy, righteous, perfect One. You are the trustworthy One. Your love is like no other. What a great love – no greater love. It would be so great for You to rapture us soon. Just think, no sickness, no dying, just meeting Jesus in the air. I do believe it. I want to be ready when the Bridegroom comes for me.

HOLY SPIRIT: Jan, I want you to learn of Me. My Word will be a lamp unto your feet. Read My Word. Study My Word. Learn of Me. Feed My sheep. Love My saints. Be an encourager to My saints.

September 30, 1999

JAN: Thank you, Father, for health. Please allow us to live our lives fully, each day to the fullest. And when it's time, let us just go, quickly and quietly, to be with You. The rapture would be great if You so choose.

HOLY SPIRIT: Jan, I will help you. Turn to Me. Turn to Me.

I will help you with the blessing and the study of the blessing.

Put all your Bibles on a shelf together. Also, any commentaries, dictionaries, etc. Also, keep all blessing materials together.

October 4, 1999

JAN: Today is a new day. Today is a new month. We need a new outpouring of Your spirit for this day. We are a needy people.

HOLY SPIRIT: I'm showing you a door. Walk into it. I must tell you to rest in Me. Don't get wound up over all you have to do, to accomplish, to make happen. Relax and let Me work through you. Don't fret, fidget. Just rest in Me. Relax – now.

HOLY SPIRIT: It's not how long you spend with Me, it's the quality of our time. In heaven we will have both quantity and quality time.

I still want you to do the blessing. It's a natural for you. I will open doors. I will show you and give you a desire for teaching the blessing and also a desire for My Word. I can change desires. I desire you for Myself. I do desire you to be healthy and happy.

I want to give you joy, happiness and peace.

Remember, he who keeps his mind on Me, I will keep in perfect peace.

Surround yourself with people who know Me and are in close contact with Me. Choose your friends well and develop them.

I will be with you in sickness and in health.
I Am.
I will make a way when there is no way.
I will keep you in perfect peace – if – your mind stays on Me.
I will deliver you. I am your Healer and Deliverer.
I am the indwelling Holy Spirit that goes with you through each day.

Right now the emphasis is not what you can do for Me. The emphasis is what the Holy Spirit can do for you. Be happy. Life is fleeting. I want you to learn and enjoy being a recipient of My blessings. You are always trying to be a blessing to others. Just let Me bless you. The blessings I give you cannot be destroyed by moths or thieves.

Monday, March 12, 2000

JAN: Father, I am still basking in Your presence. Thank You for Your presence and your Holy Spirit. I love You. I want a love relationship with You. Please, Lord, keep pursuing me. I praise Your

Name. I glorify (make splendid) all Your works. You are my faithful and true God. I can trust you as my best Friend. I can lean on You. Your Word is true. Your promises to me are true.

You will heal all my diseases. You can give me joy unspeakable and full of glory (splendor). Faithful and true = trustworthy

You know my physical needs
        my spiritual needs
        my emotional needs
        my financial needs

You are the source of all I need. First, I need a love relationship that is ongoing with You.

Today the Holy Spirit is so real. I am so honored to have the Holy Spirit visit and stay with me today. He brings a sweet peace. I wish I could feel His presence so real, always.

As I look at Thomas Kinkade's calendar picture for March, God seems to be relating this picture to the afterlife. It is the garden picture dominated by white concrete steps and flowers, trees and greenery.

It seems as though this is the transition walk to the afterlife. We are at the bottom of the steps, standing in the green grass. When the time comes, God will send an angel to walk with us up the steps and into that hazy, beautiful garden which we can't really see. That is heaven or the beginning path to heaven.

This is the peace I give, not as the world giveth. Peace that passes all understanding. Peace, perfect peace. This is the kind of peace my sister, Bonnie, had. No cares, worries, just peace. She said, "I am in God's hands. I have peace."

HOLY SPIRIT: Be still and know that I am God. I will fill your cup to overflowing. Your needs are met before you voice them. I will meet all your needs according to My riches in glory. I AM all you need. Be sure you have a love relationship with Me. I can bring all things to your remembrance. I can meet you at your point of need. I touched you. I continue to touch and heal you. You can read the health books, but I'm healing you without them.

April 16, 2001

HOLY SPIRIT: Jan, I am not going to take you now. You still need to be here. You still have a purpose. I want to renew your mind; your thought process. Think on these things – the blessing . . . you're holding on to it like a diamond. Release it – share it – study it. Don't hold onto it. Open your hands and give it to others.

July 18, 2001

HOLY SPIRIT: You feel so ashamed that you have accomplished so little.

Don't do something – stand there. Don't lose heart. Don't lose faith. I am strong. I am your Deliverer. I am your Healer. I am your Provider. I am what you need.

JAN: Yes, Jesus took my burdens I could no longer bear. Yes, Jesus took my burdens in answer to my prayer. My anxious fears subsided. My spirit was made strong. For Jesus took my burdens and left me with a song.

HOLY SPIRIT: Release it all! Release it all to Me. I am your source of strength, of health, of wealth, of contentment, of happiness.

Let Me minister to you. Let Me fill you with My Spirit to flow through you. You cannot allow this and still be in control.

Pray and trust and obey. Trust and obey, for there's no other way, to be happy in Jesus, than to trust and obey.

You are not in control. Nothing you can do will change that. You are not responsible – it is not your responsibility – it is Mine. Don't try to be Me.

I am the one that works miracles, not you. I am the Provider, not you. I am their source of strength, not you.

Janice, please talk to Me – all day – every day. Tell Me your concerns. Don't try to solve everything yourself. You are on overload. Give it all to Me. Bring Me your cares, concerns and problems. I am the great Fixer! I can fix problems! I can solve problems! I can do great and mighty works! I am also interested in you and your problems. Yes, I will help you.

Just praise Me and allow Me to work in your life. You don't have to see what's coming. You don't have to plan it. You don't have to make it happen. You don't have to think, if it's to be, it's up to me. No it is not!

Nothing is up to you. I am in control. You gave yourself to Me. I am controlling now. I am your Captain. You relax and enjoy the cruise. I know the seas, the rocks, the winds. I am in control.

If you try to be all things to all people, you cannot. If you take responsibilities in your hands, you cannot. If you try to solve all problems, you cannot. That is MY JOB, JANICE. Your job is to love, bless, rejoice, praise, and delight in Me and your family. I am your Abba Father. I take care of your needs. Can you ever relax in Me and just enjoy the journey?

We are on course. Now don't come take the wheel from Me. You do not know the way. You do not know the winds, the charts, the rocks, the straits, the dangers. Let Me guide you safely home. Let Me be your Captain.

For three years I've asked you to study the blessing. Seek ye first the kingdom of God and His righteousness, and all these things will be added unto you.

I demand first place. If I tell you to do something, that comes first. Just study the blessing. That's all I ask right now.

I know you are sorry for disobedience, and I forgive you and I give you another chance. But please, Janice, do My will. Everything else must go – no matter what it is.

Pace yourself so you don't get over-tired and over-burdened. You are no longer twenty-five. You deserve some rest. Don't feel guilty when you rest. Don't feel guilty when you don't do all the things on your list. Let Me in on your life. Let Me help you.

Don't think – well, I can take care of this by myself. Just allow Me to be with you on every decision.

October 25, 2002

JAN: I am teaching the blessing.

HOLY SPIRIT: Be still and know that I am God. I am the One who gave you promises in My Word. I am able to make them come true. Be thankful and bless My name. I am your Healer. Yes, I am healing you. I am Bob's Healer. Yes, I am healing Bob. Jan, I know your needs. You want to "fix" everything and everybody. Just let Me fix things and people. Enjoy today. Have faith in tomorrow. Have faith in Me.

Easter Sunday 2003

HOLY SPIRIT: I just want to tell you, today, just how much I love you. I love you, Jan. I will protect you. I will hold you in the palm of My hand. I will heal your sicknesses. I will heal your diseases. You are benign. You trust in Me and My Word. My Word does not return void. My words are alive. My words are life.

Jan, I want you to leave fear. I want you to put on faith and walk in

40

faith that your Father loves you and will heal you and take care of you.

Enjoy and rejoice in this holy day. Know that I am with you. Talk to Me. Sense My spirit with you. I want quiet times with you. I want to reveal some things to you. Read My Word – that's how you understand Me. Talk with Me – that's how the love relationship develops. Hope in Me – I am the way, the truth, the life. No man comes to the Father, except by Me. Let Me handle the big deal. You handle the little things – read, pray, and spend time with Me.

June 7, 2003

JAN: Lord, I want to listen to you.

HOLY SPIRIT: Jan, I am in control. You can stand on your head but I am still in control. You can't make it happen. I can and will heal all of your sicknesses and diseases. It is done! Don't get uptight and short out your being. Just open up and let Me flow through you. I will help you. I will take care of you. Laugh, be happy. I will give you focus and concentration. I'm talking to you. This is the most important part of the day – My time with you.

JAN: It is so exciting to see how God is directing our lives. He is ordering our steps, just like we prayed for Him to do. Sometimes, I feel like I'm a little puppet and God is in charge, not I! Oh, I know we have a will and we can choose our own way. But, when I found out I had cancer, I turned the strings of my life over to Him. So I, by my own volition, asked Him to take charge of my life. He has been so faithful. I feel like everywhere I go, God puts someone in my life for a purpose.

September 8, 2004

JAN: Oh, Lord, O Lord how Majestic is your name in all the earth. Oh, Lord, You are forever glorious. You are patient and kind. You are faithful. You are my rock and salvation. Oh, how I love You. God is good – all the time. You are faithful in the good times. You are faithful in the bad times. How close You are today. Your Holy Spirit is so near. Your peace covers me as a blanket. Your love enfolds me. You are great! And greatly to be praised! I thank You for my life.

HOLY SPIRIT: Just rest in Me. I am not finished with you and Bob and your lives. I will give you years to make a difference in the lives of others.

You are Mine. You are bought with a price. Oh, what a price I paid for you. Never think My love is small or shallow. My love is great and all compassing. My love for you is without reservation. You do not have to qualify for My love. You do not have to deserve it. You do not have to earn it. I loved you before you were born and I paid a price for you before you were ever born. Please accept My love as a gift. Do not think that My love is for everyone else, but not you. This is a problem for you.

Now, just know you are loved by Me. If you cannot identify with a father's love, can you identify with your husband's love? It is godly love. You know and can accept Bob's love. Just accept My love and know I will do anything and everything to make you well and whole again. If you ask for a good gift, such as healing, you know I will not give you bad things, don't you? So, ask for health, knowing I delight in giving gifts to My children.

And I am pleased with you, Jan. I am glad you draw near to ME in times of trouble or despair. I will hold you in the palm of My hand. I will cover you with My wings of protection. I will shield you from the enemy and the storms. You are Mine. Do you understand that? In being My child, I am responsible for your well-being. I enjoy working out your future. I enjoy planning things for you.

It is My job, and My joy, to love and take care of My children. Every father is a provider. I am the Great Provider. I provide all your needs, according to My riches in glory. I have great riches. I have great abundance. You, with the Power of the Holy Spirit, can tap into My sources.

As My child, you have an inheritance. You inherit My provisions. There is never lack in My storehouse. Now, update your prayer list. I will honor you and give you peace. Go, now with My peace and blessing.

Take a quiet time every day with Me. We will accomplish great things during that time. Lean on Me for support and guidance. You are Mine. You are bought with a great price. I treasure you.

September 14, 2004

HOLY SPIRIT: Jan, you had polio – which brought you to Me. Since then, you have been greatly blessed.

I gave you Bob, the most wonderful partner in the world. I gave you two sons, who love Me and are great men. You and Bob have always succeeded in everything. A strong marriage, a strong family, a strong faith. Others looked at you with envy. You never had problems. You wore beautiful clothes, drove nice cars, looked and acted like you had everything. And indeed, you did. They were My blessings to you. I did not allow you to have cancer when you were young and your children were young. But, you need to be a witness for Me that is relatable. Now, everyone sees your challenge. Everyone who meets you knows you have a cane for a reason. They know you had breast cancer.

Now, I can use you in a more dynamic way. You are faithful to give Me credit. You have a new capacity to love, to care, to be grateful, to be thankful.

You have grown in your prayer life. You pray for others in intercessory prayer.

I want this for you.

Yes, everyone will have challenges.

Yours is a refining process so that you may glorify your Father which is in heaven.

April 9, 2006

JAN: Lord, I want to hear from You.

HOLY SPIRIT: You will be given extended life to do My work – not yours. You must focus on ME and My work. Half of your day should be spent that way. The other half is for you. Worship is for Me. Other things are for you.

I want you to study the blessing. I want to give to you and your family great blessings. I want you to produce fruit. I want you to say the High Priestly Blessing to those who come through your doors. I want you to begin blessing those you love – bless them using examples in the Word. Bless children when you have the opportunity. Use the blessing daily. Make it a part of your life.

JAN: Is the blessing done just at special times?

HOLY SPIRIT: It is done at special times – when you depart from your loved ones as I did when I left My disciples to ascend into heaven. The first-born blessing was a very important and special blessing. Esau sold his birthright for a bowl of soup. But, I blessed the children when I had the opportunity. Don't miss opportunities to let children come to you to be blessed.

I do have a hope and a future for you. Your future is filled with the Holy Spirit upon you if you follow Me daily. Spend time with Me. This is a project I will help you through. It will be an exciting journey!

I am coming soon! Time is precious. Write a book about your healing experience. Include healing scriptures in the book. It will take faith to do this. I need you to do this. Explain your verses on healing being the will of God.

JAN: Lord – all this takes time. I am busy now. Where do I find the time? Please help me with this.

HOLY SPIRIT: You are so blessed. You have My word. You have faith in Me. I am going to reward you. I am constantly healing you. You are a vessel. You and Bob are vessels. You are actually mentoring now. You need the Holy Spirit daily in a mighty way. Your Bible studies – you see Me working, don't you? Start your book.

JAN: I am really enjoying studying the blessing.

You are here today, God.

I am outside on the deck with You. It is so beautiful out here.

HOLY SPIRIT: Jan, Jan, you are Mine. Your days and nights will be filled with My presence. I send the Holy Spirit to dwell in you. I will send power from on high. You will have renewed strength and renewed youth – you and Bob. Be joyful! Be happy! Be loving!

Note from Author: Below is my favorite conversation Jan had with God.

Monday, April 10, 2006

HOLY SPIRIT: I am excited that you are studying the blessing. You got up at 4:00 a.m. this morning to study and be with Me. I have been looking forward to our time together. I will bless you for that, Janice.

Now, be sure to end with prayer and the High Priestly Blessing tonight after the Bible study.

Now, yesterday, Jan, we agreed you would spend two hours studying the blessing, but you didn't – why?

JAN: Well, God, I am sorry, but I got busy with some of Bob's needs, and some other things!

HOLY SPIRIT: Well, Jan, what is more important – Bob or Me? Other things – or Me?

I have not blessed everyone as I have blessed you. You know that. I commune with you. I speak to you. I gave you Bob and your sons. I allowed cancer to come upon you for My glory. I have healed you and you have a testimony – a testimony to share with others. Now you must study and share the blessing. Seek out sources and make them your own. Keep it simple. The spoken Word is so powerful.

Write a blessing. Frame it and give it. But SPEAK it over them when you are with them. Think and pray about the blessing for each one.

Jan, you asked for My peace last night. Today I bestow upon you My everlasting peace. You will notice a difference in your frustration level and your joy will return. Just praise Me in the good times and in the bad times.

Jan, this is My day – Sunday – the Sabbath. Dedicate the entire day to Me. I will restore your peace and joy. Have a Blessed Day!

JAN: How will I use the blessing daily?

HOLY SPIRIT: You can always use the High Priestly Blessing. You can write out blessings, as you have done in the past. Keep it simple for others to follow. You may concentrate on one or two things. Be sure you read and understand that you are not the "Blesser." Explain that to people when you bless them. Study this point so it is clear in your mind. The blessing is a type of prayer.

August 24, 2007

HOLY SPIRIT: You know I have all the time in the world. I have eternity. You have time on this earth. You need to organize your time. Seek Me each day to help you.

Great and glorious things will I do through you. You are yielded to Me. I want to flow through you. I want you as My vessel.

The secret is the Holy Spirit living in you, blessing you, surrounding you with love and protection, yes, and drawing good things to you.

You are blessed. You are blessed going out and coming in. You shall be in a bubble of blessing. No weapon formed against you shall prosper. You are untouchable to the enemy. He is not allowed on your turf.

Chapter Six
Thirty Qualities for Dating

Bob, age 17   Jan, age 16

WOW!!! Was I the "lucky" guy – no, the honored boy to find, date, and marry Janice Marie Brown.

Jan was so special and close to God since she gave her life to Jesus at age twelve on a polio bed. Doctors said she would never be normal, walk, or have children. Her left side was paralyzed, but she prayed to God for healing and committed her life to Him. He did heal her, praise God, and she lived an abundantly full life as a Christian, wife, and mother of two boys. She was absolutely the best wife and mother possible. She always did her best to encourage me, support me, and meet all my needs, always.

Jan prayerfully made this list of thirty qualities of the man she knew God wanted her to marry. She was sixteen when she made this list. After every date, Jan would take the list out of her Bible and check it. She had already said no to three marriage proposals before I even dated her. Fortunately, none of them qualified. YEA!!! But I did, at least for most of them! Thank God!!!

Use Jan's list, or your own, for dating. Jan would tell you that this is the second most important decision one makes in life.

This is a picture of Jan and me on Valentine's Day, February 14, 1956, the night I asked Jan to "go steady."

Desirable Qualities or Characteristics for Dating

1. Spiritual
2. Mature
3. Self-confident; sure of himself
4. Masculine; gives me a feeling of security
5. Interested in the same things I am
6. Sincere and deep
7. Good personality
   a. Likes people
   b. Has friends
   c. Isn't cutting
   d. Doesn't think he's perfect
8. Spiritual leader
9. Kind, understanding, and considerate
10. Straightforward, frank, and honest
11. True to his word
12. Capable of making own decisions; doesn't act on impulses
13. Enjoyable to be around; never dull or tiring; just plain exciting!
14. Makes me feel proud and happy to be with him
15. Doesn't tell all his business
16. Doesn't gripe and complain, but faces life with a smile; cheerful
17. Doesn't try to fool me or pretend; I should know his real self
18. Doesn't humor or baby me, but acknowledges that I'm capable of doing things myself
19. Not fast
20. Not bossy; doesn't tell me what to do
21. Doesn't flirt; is true
22. Is patient
23. Isn't jealous
24. Isn't stingy
25. Isn't selfish
26. Doesn't talk unjustly about people
27. Should have common sense
28. Likes me for what I am
29. Makes me feel at ease with him and his friends
30. Sees and loves my spiritual and inner being

These are the Thirty Qualities in
Jan's own handwriting.

Desirable Qualities or Characteristics

1. Spiritual
2. Mature
3. Self confident; sure of himself
4. Masculine; gives me a feeling of security.
5. Interested in the same things I am
6. Sincere and deep
7. Good personality
   a. likes people
   b. has friends
   c. isn't cutting
   d. doesn't think he's perfect
8. Spiritual leader
9. Kind, understanding and considerate

10. Straightforward, frank, and honest.
11. True to his word
12. Capable of making own decisions, doesn't act on impulses.
13. Enjoyable to be around, never dull or tiring, just plain exciting.
14. Makes me feel proud and happy to be with him.
15. Doesn't tell all he knows
16. Doesn't gripe and complain but faces life with a smile. Cheerful.
17. Doesn't try to fool me or pretend. I should know his real self.

18. Doesn't humor or baby me, but acknowledges that I'm capable of doing things myself.
19. Not fast
20. Not bossy. Doesn't tell me what to do.
21. Doesn't flirt. Is true.
22. Is patient
23. Isn't jealous
24. Isn't stingy
25. Isn't selfish
26. Doesn't talk ugly about people.
27. Should have common sense.
28. Likes me for what I am
29. Makes me feel at ease with him & his friends
30. Sees & loves my spiritual and inner being.

51

Bob and Jan's
wedding invitation

Mr. and Mrs. Joseph Bannard Brown

request the honour of your presence

at the marriage of their daughter

Janice Marie

to

Mr. Robert Frederick Fraumann

on Saturday, the first of June

nineteen hundred and fifty-seven

at eight o'clock in the evening

Sanctified Church of Christ

Columbus, Georgia

Reception
immediately following the ceremony

Chapter Seven

The Legacy of a Fraumann

Fraumanns are different

Fraumanns are special

Fraumanns are loved by God and blessed by God

Fraumanns don't say what we don't like—we say what we like

Fraumanns are not quitters—we finish what we start

Fraumanns take care of and stand by one another

Fraumanns go to church to worship the Lord and keep the Sabbath EVERY Sunday

Fraumanns have a tender heart toward God

Fraumanns are good looking

Fraumanns are gifted by God and have many talents

Fraumanns love people

Fraumanns are leaders

Fraumanns believe a person's character is more important than their qualifications

Fraumanns ask and receive God's protection

Fraumanns have a Christian heritage

Fraumanns are hardworking—they work twice as hard as most people

Fraumanns set goals for their lives, and work to achieve them, with God's help

Fraumanns have a great purpose for their lives

Fraumanns look for the positive, believing that in every adversity, there is a seed of overcoming

There has never been a lazy Fraumann

The Fraumann heritage is, "You can believe and trust a Fraumann. Their word is their bond"

The Fraumann laugh, smile and sense of humor is a legend.

Signed: Jan Fraumann, 1993

Chapter Eight
Love Letters

Jan and I wrote love letters daily (over two hundred) during our two and one-half year courtship and engagement. We had a special relationship and understanding. As we grew in our love, we respected each other, and intentionally kept our dating a God-like dating experience. It was very passionate, and therefore we prayed before, during, and after dates.

During our courtship, I traveled all over the U.S with three other teenagers, George Morris, Bob Carpenter, and Jerry Dooling, for two and one-half years. We traveled over forty thousand miles, through twenty-four states, holding over fifty revivals, and witnessed over six hundred and fifty people make decisions for Christ in their lives. We traveled an average of five hundred miles weekly, before highway interstates.

As you read through these excerpts from our more than two hundred letters, notice not only our growing love for each other, but how our love of God was the basis and support of our relationship.

You will experience our relationship with God, His blessings on our dating, and serving Him to win people to Him through our lives, example, and music.

Jan to Bob

Dearest Sweetheart,

I'm so lonesome for you tonight. It's been two whole days since I've seen you. There is a closeness between us that I've never experienced before. I believe that our love is a deep, steady love, one that's deep and sure. It reminds me so much of the love of God. My heart thrills when I remember how we started out – with the Lord. Honey, I want it always to be that way. I consider your love the biggest blessing God has given me, next to my salvation. It makes me want to serve the Lord more and live as close to Him as I can. Isn't it wonderful to be a Christian, Bob? What would we ever do without the Lord? Honey, I'm so thankful for your wonderful Christian life! You'll never know what a blessing you've been to your girlfriend. You've been so kind and understanding so many times. Your life has always been spotless and giving. To me, you're just the type of Christian I'd like to be. I love you, Darling, with all my heart.

With all my love,
Jan

First Corinthians 13:12 (KJV)
For now we see through a glass, darkly; but then face to face: now I know in part; but then shall I know even as also I am known.

BOB TO JAN

MY DEAREST, PRECIOUS, SWEETEST, DARLING, JANICE,

IT THRILLS ME TO KNOW THAT OUR LOVE IS CHRIST CENTERED, AND THAT EVERYTHING WE DO OR SAY HAS CHRIST AS ITS ULTIMATE GOAL. IF WE LET CHRIST ALWAYS HAVE COMPLETE AND PERFECT CONTROL OF OUR LIVES, AS HE HAS SO FAR, THEN WE CAN ALWAYS HAVE THE GOOD ASSURANCE THAT HE IS GOING TO WORK OUT EVERYTHING IN OUR LIVES. I HAVE SO MUCH LOVE STORED UP IN MY HEART FOR YOU. I CAN HARDLY WAIT TO BE WITH YOU. WE HAVE SO MANY GOOD MEMORIES TO LOOK BACK OVER AND THANK THE LORD FOR. I ALWAYS LIKE TO THINK OF OUR PRAYING TOGETHER EVERY DAY. WE ALWAYS TOOK TIME OUT EVERY DAY FOR THE LORD AND WE ALWAYS WILL WHEN WE'RE TOGETHER. IN FACT, WE STILL DO WHEN WE'RE APART, AT OUR REGULAR HOUR WE PICKED EACH EVENING.

REMEMBER, WHEN I ASKED YOU TO "GO STEADY" AND WE DECIDED TO PRAY ABOUT IT. WE DID PRAY THAT WEEKEND AND ON MONDAY STARTED "GOING STEADY." THAT'S WHEN THE SPARK LIT. THE SPARK OF LOVE STARTED BURNING AND CHRIST STARTED IT AND HE WILL KEEP IT BURNING. ALL I CAN SAY IS, "THANK YOU, LORD, FOR ALL YOUR BLESSINGS. I LOVE YOU AND THE BEAUTIFUL, CHRISTIAN GIRL YOU GAVE ME."

I WANT YOU TO CONTINUE TO PRAY WITH ME THAT GOD'S RICHEST BLESSINGS MAY BE OURS, AND THAT HE WILL GUIDE US AS A COUPLE.

ALL MY LOVE, ALWAYS,
BOB

FIRST CORINTHIANS 15:57-58 (KJV)
BUT THANKS BE TO GOD, WHICH GIVETH US THE VICTORY
THROUGH OUR LORD JESUS CHRIST. THEREFORE, MY
BELOVED BRETHREN, BE YE STEADFAST, UNMOVABLE,
ALWAYS ABOUNDING IN THE WORK OF THE LORD, FOR AS
MUCH AS YE KNOW THAT YOUR LABOUR IS NOT IN VAIN IN
THE LORD.

Jan to Bob

My Dearest Sweetheart,

Honey, it's always romantic when I am with you. Honey, I hope we never change because I want us always to be romantic and sentimental, and always tender and understanding.

So many people have told me that I don't know what I'm getting into – that married life soon gets the same – that you are tied down. But, Bob, I want us to be different – to always be lovers. I want us to be happy all the time and be understanding and considerate. Honey, I want you to mean twenty-five million times more (in twenty-five years) than what you mean to me now.

I love you! I want you always to remember it too, Bob! For you're all I've dreamed, hoped, and prayed for. Honey, you're my everything. I want you to know what a sweet boyfriend you have been to me.

Even though we have been apart while you are traveling in revivals, our love hasn't stopped growing. I now realize how much you mean to me –

how happy I am with you, and how incomplete I am without you. I'm desperately in love with you, and Honey, this is my promise; I always will be.

Bob, I never in my life dreamed I could be as close to any boy as I am to you. You seem to understand me even when I don't understand myself. I love you just the way you are. I feel that our love is based on a real foundation. First, it's based on the will of God. Then we've found love and understanding that has grown daily. I want our lives and our love to always have Christ as the center. That's the secret of happiness. And we have found much happiness, haven't we?

And Darling, I want to tell you how proud I am of you for the work you've been doing for the Lord in revivals. It means so much to me to know you're completely His. I'm anxious to pray with you again, for I think I've missed that more than anything.
My love forever,
Janice

Luke 1:37 (KJV)
For with God nothing shall be impossible.

BOB TO JAN

MY DEAREST JAN,

I LOVE YOU, DARLING, WITH A LOVE THAT'S WAY DOWN DEEP INSIDE AND ETERNAL, NEVER-DYING, DEEP, REAL, LOVE THAT'S ALL YOURS FROM ME, 'CAUSE I LOVE YOU WITH ALL MY HEART AND ALWAYS WILL WITH A DEEP CONSECRATED, SACRED CHRISTIAN LOVE.

GOD HAS SO WONDERFULLY AND RICHLY BLESSED US TOGETHER, I CAN TRUTHFULLY SAY. I AM SO PLEASED WITH OUR COURTSHIP AND DATING. IT HAS BEEN CLEAN AND PURE. I HAVE LOVED EVERY MINUTE OF IT WITH NO REGRETS, BECAUSE WE HAVE ALWAYS STAYED IN HIS WILL. I'M THRILLED BECAUSE WE ARE ONLY ONE OF MANY COUPLES WHO HAVE KEPT CHRIST AS THE CENTER OF THEIR DATING. WE ARE IN MINISTRY AS A CHRISTIAN COUPLE — AND COMPARED TO THE WORLD — IF OTHER COUPLES HAD THIS LOVE IN THEIR HEARTS FOR GOD AND EACH OTHER AS WE DO — THERE WOULD BE MANY MORE HAPPIER HOMES. AS FAR AS WE'RE CONCERNED, WE'RE GOING TO BE AN EXAMPLE AS A CHRISTIAN COUPLE, SO OTHERS CAN SEE THAT WE'RE COMPLETELY SATISFIED WITH GOD AND LOVE HIM. WE KNOW HE LOVES US AND WORKS OUT OUR LIVES AS HE SEES FIT.

MY LOVE ALWAYS,
BOB

PHILIPPIANS 1:3-4 (KJV)
I THANK MY GOD UPON EVERY REMEMBRANCE OF YOU, ALWAYS IN EVERY PRAYER OF MINE FOR YOU ALL MAKING REQUEST WITH JOY.

Jan to Bob

Dear Bob,

I am really and truly in love with you. The wonderful thing about it is that I'm happy and peaceful inside and believe with all my heart that it's right. I feel the presence of the Lord — I feel His guiding hand on our lives; almost too wonderful to be true. Bob, I want our love to be "the best." And why can't it be, if we love each other and always keep God first in everything. There's nothing any sweeter to me that the bond <u>we</u> have through prayer. It means so much to know that <u>you</u> are praying for me. It gives me that extra little "boost" I need, for I know that God hears and answers your prayers. Bob, if I went on and on forever, I'd never really be able to tell you the real love and feeling I have for you. It's like the love of God and our love to Him — it's inexplainable. I'm incapable of expressing myself. All I can tell you is that from the bottom of my heart "I love you."

Jan

John 15:16 (KJV)

Ye have not chosen me, but I have chosen you, and ordained you, that ye should go and bring forth fruit, and that your fruit should remain: that whatsoever ye shall ask of the Father in my name, he may give it you.

Psalm 37:3-5 (KJV)

Trust in the LORD, and do good; so shalt thou dwell in the land, and verily thou shalt be fed. Delight thyself also in the LORD: and He shall give thee the desires of thine heart. Commit thy way unto the LORD; trust also in him; and He shall bring it to pass.

P.S. Pennsylvania has one thing that Georgia doesn't, I'll admit, and that is the most handsome, most understanding, sweetest, and greatest guy I've ever known. Yep, he's the one I love and the state doesn't matter one bit.

BOB TO JAN

MY DEAREST JANICE,

I CAN HARDLY WAIT TO SEE YOU. YOU'RE SO SWEET AND LOVING, AND A PRAYING CHRISTIAN WIFE-TO-BE, WHO WILL SOON BE MINE, FOREVER.

I'M RECOVERING TODAY IN THE HOSPITAL FROM MY TONSILLECTOMY. THERE ARE FOUR IN MY ROOM. ALL ARE FRIENDLY, BUT SWEAR A LOT. I CAN'T TALK, SO I DON'T KNOW HOW TO WITNESS TO THEM — SO, I TURNED ON MY RADIO WITH GOSPEL MUSIC AND LET THEM KNOW, AT LEAST, HOW I BELIEVE.

I LOVE YOU, DARLING, SO MUCH. YOU ARE MY DREAM COME TRUE. JUST FIVE AND ONE-HALF MONTHS TILL WE ARE MARRIED. MY PRAYER IS THAT WE WILL BOTH BE COMPLETELY HAPPY — AND I CAN BE THE KIND OF HUSBAND YOU WANT AND NEED, BECAUSE YOU ARE MY DREAM COME TRUE.

ALL MY LOVE, JUST FOR YOU,
BOB

FIRST CORINTHIANS 3:23 (KJV)
AND YE ARE CHRIST'S; AND CHRIST IS GOD'S.

Jan to Bob

Hi, My Honey Darling,

I love you so much. I've never had one doubt about my love for you, and that's the way it's always gonna be. You're the only one I've ever loved or even could love. You're the sweetest, kindest, most understanding and best guy in the world, and, Honey, I'm the luckiest and most blessed girl in the world to call you my own. Your love means more to me than you'll ever know. All I can say, Honey, is that I love you and I'm happy and more than satisfied with our love. I never realized love could be so wonderful and real. I've just never been in love before. You're my one and only — always!

You know — before you told me you loved me you asked me if I thought we were in the Lord's will dating each other. I had already prayed much about us, and I felt in the Lord's will and happy. Well, I feel so much happier and content now. You said it so sweetly — that it seemed that the Lord had put His seal of approval on us. You know, I don't know another couple at Asbury (on campus) that God has blessed more than He has us. I am so unworthy of such love and blessing. But, we are determined to serve Him, huh-darling?

Bob, your letters and talks to me about spiritual things have helped me so much. There's just nothing that can help me like my Bob. I praise the Lord for such a wonderful, Christian sweetheart.

I'm so anxious to pray with you once again. Those times mean so much to me.

I love you, darling,
Janice

Matthew 28:19-20 (KJV)
Go ye therefore, and teach all nations, baptizing them in the name of the Father, and of the Son, and of the Holy Ghost: Teaching them to observe all things whatsoever I have commanded you: and, lo, I am with you always, even unto the end of the world. Amen.

BOB TO JAN

TO MY SWEETHEART, MY LOVE,

I AM LOVE-SICK OVER YOU. HONEY, I AM SO THANKFUL FOR THE LORD GIVING YOU TO ME. I HAVE THOUGHT MUCH ABOUT YOU AND OUR COURTSHIP. I HAVE PRAYED ABOUT IT AND FEEL WE ARE SO MUCH IN THE LORD'S WILL. YOU ARE MINE ALWAYS AND FOREVER, AND GOD HAS PUT HIS SEAL OF APPROVAL ON US.

BECAUSE I LOVE GOD FIRST – I BELIEVE GOD SAW THE SWEETEST, MOST UNDERSTANDING, WONDERFUL, CONSIDERATE, LOVING, LOVABLE, PRECIOUS, BEAUTIFUL, DARLING GEORGIA PEACH AND SAID, "BOB, I HAVE A GIFT FOR YOU THAT YOU CAN ENJOY THE REST OF YOUR LIFE. SHE IS SOMEONE WHO LOVES GOD, LOVES THE CHURCH, AND ALSO HAS A BURDEN FOR SOULS. SHE WILL BACK YOU UP IN PRAYER LIKE YOU HAVE NEVER KNOWN BEFORE."

I'M HAPPY, JAN, THAT YOU THRILL ME, AND I KNOW THAT AS I AM OUT HERE TRAVELING, DOING THIS FOR THE SAME GOD THAT GAVE YOU TO ME, THAT HE IS GOING TO BLESS OUR LOVE AND MAKE IT THRIVE AND GROW.

BEFORE I STARTED DATING YOU, I HEARD MORE COMPLIMENTS FROM FRIENDS AND FAMILY ABOUT YOUR DEVOTION TO GOD AND YOUR LOVE FOR HIM. YOU KNOW WE DON'T HAVE TO TELL WHAT IS IN OUR HEARTS – IT WILL SHOW IN OUR LIVES, DARLING. YOUR LIFE TO ME HAS THE SPARKLE OF CHRISTIAN LIVING WATER FLOWING AND BLESSING OTHERS. IT SURELY BLESSES ME.

MY LOVE ALWAYS & FOREVER,
BOB

PSALM 23:1 (KJV)
THE LORD IS MY SHEPHERD; I SHALL NOT WANT.

Janice Fraumann

Jan to Bob

Hi Honey,

    I miss you so much and miss so much praying together. Your sweet and sincere prayers have meant so much in my Christian life. I'm still the Lord's girl, Honey, and then next, I'm your girl. I'm really proud of the way we treat each other. Be sweet and you can be sure I'm thinking about you every minute cause . . .

I love you,
Janice

BOB TO JAN

DARLING,

    WE HAVE GOOD CHRISTIAN FUN AND FELLOWSHIP TOGETHER ON OUR DATES. I'M LOOKING FORWARD TO SEVENTY-FIVE MORE YEARS TOGETHER, BECAUSE, DARLING, I LOVE YOU WITH ALL MY HEART.

    I LOVE YOU, DARLING, WITH ALL MY HEART AND WILL BE YOURS THROUGHOUT MY LIFETIME FOREVER AND EVER AS YOUR HUSBAND. YOU'RE SO SWEET AND I ADORE YOU AND NEED YOU TO BE ALL MINE — MY SWEET WIFE.

I LOVE YOU,
BOB

(NOTE: JAN LIVED TO BE SEVENTY-FIVE YEARS AND FIVE DAYS.)

Jan to Bob

My Sweet, Precious, Darling Sweetheart,

I love you this morning!! I slept with your picture under my pillow. I want to be near you so badly.

I don't really feel like I have a heart, but the place where it was just aches. But, Darling, you have my heart and I'm so glad you do, for I have no need for it.

Sweetheart, I feel that you miss me, too, and it comforts my heart to know beyond a shadow of a doubt that "Bob loves me."

You are the sweetest boy in all the world, and you know what? I'm the luckiest girl in all the world!! I'm in love with you, Darling, and I never want you to forget it.

Sweetheart, I feel that the Lord is really using you this summer. I want to do my part for Him <u>and you</u>, by praying for you constantly.

I wrote a note to your parents and will write them often. I know they miss you so much and sympathize with me. I love them so much.

I believe the Lord will bless us. I believe He smiles on us as a couple. We started out with Him. I've never been sorry for a thing we've done. We've kept our dating clean and pure.

Now, God needs you and wants to use you to help the lost, unsaved, unhappy world, so that others might enjoy the love of Jesus as we do.

We want to share with others who need God. So many need Him, and so few who are willing. I want us to always be willing. I'm praying that He'll make me more willing to sing for Him. I want to keep the joy of Jesus in my heart and keep our Jesus first!

I'll always love you,
Jan

Philippians 1:21 (KJV)
For to me to live is Christ, and to die is gain.

BOB TO JAN

MY DEAREST DARLING,

I LOVE YOU SO MUCH AND WANT YOU TO KNOW THAT TWELVE WEEKS FROM TODAY, WE'LL BE MARRIED. DARLING, I TOLD THE LORD THIS MORNING I'M GOING TO TRUST HIM COMPLETELY IN THIS, BECAUSE I FEEL IN HIS WILL AND KNOW HE'LL WORK EVERYTHING OUT. HE HAS BROUGHT US TOGETHER AND LED US TO MARRIAGE. NOW, WE WANT TO SERVE HIM AND DO HIS WILL. JUST THINK, WE WILL BE TOGETHER THE REST OF OUR LIVES SERVING CHRIST.

ALL MY LOVE, FOREVER,

BOB

PHILIPPIANS 4:19 (KJV)
BUT MY GOD SHALL SUPPLY ALL YOUR NEED ACCORDING TO HIS RICHES IN GLORY BY CHRIST JESUS.

Jan to Bob

My Dearest Lover,

It is wonderful to hear about the conversions in Mississippi, and now in South Carolina. Honey, I wouldn't have you doing anything but the Lord's work – I'm so proud of you, and the way you're working for Him this summer.

I'm really and truly in love with you, and it's wonderful to be content, knowing you've found what you've been looking for, and can just praise the Lord for it.

I feel a Christian worker of any kind has to be <u>deep</u> and <u>filled</u> with His presence constantly in order to be of any help or assistance to others.

I can grow as much as I want. The Lord gives me new light each day, and it's up to me to walk in it. He has confidence in us. And we decide on determining whether we fail Him, or not. I don't want to fail Him. But, I want Him to be pleased with me.

I love you and God so much, I don't want to hurt either one of you. Having both of you has made my life happy, and content, and complete.

Honey, I'm the Lord's girl and I've promised to serve Him, and I'm compelled to keep it. I've promised Him _my life_ devoted to His will. And although I don't know the future, nor what He has planned for me, I know He holds my hand, and, you know, whenever I go through joy, pain, sadness, heartache, or whatever – He still holds my hand. I love Him, Honey, and He seems more personal than ever before when I see the way He's worked in our lives. I do feel unworthy of such love, but I intend to live for Him, and do His will.

I love your name, Fraumann. I love everything about you. Seriously, I like it. It's sort of fascinating. I love you with all my heart. You mean more to me than anything or anybody, except, our partner, Jesus.

"The devil will give you a good time, but in the end he'll pay you with counterfeit money."

My love, always & forever,
Janice

Matthew 9:37 (KJV)
Then saith He unto his disciples, The harvest truly is plenteous, but the labourers are few.

72

BOB TO JAN

HI HONEY,

I LOVE YOU! I SAW THE FULL MOON TONIGHT AND IT MADE ME LONESOME FOR YOU. REMEMBER, THE FULL MOON ON CAMPUS, THE FULL MOON AT YOUR HOME, AND THE FULL MOON IN TALLAHASSEE AT THE REVIVAL?

I JUST LOVE TO THINK BACK ON OUR COURTSHIP AND SEE HOW MUCH FUN AND FELLOWSHIP WE HAD TOGETHER <u>IN CHRIST</u>. HOW THE LORD HAS BLESSED US TOGETHER! I LOOK FORWARD TO THE WAY HE'S GOING TO BLESS US. IT WILL BE WONDERFUL, 'CAUSE I FEEL WE ARE IN THE CENTER OF GOD'S WILL. THIS IS JUST THE BEGINNING.

ALL MY LOVE ALWAYS,
BOB

PHILIPPIANS 4:13 (KJV)
I CAN DO ALL THINGS THROUGH CHRIST WHICH STRENGTH-ENETH ME.

Letters ~ 2005

Here are three letters Jan wrote to me

2005 – Forty-seven years later
2013 – Fifty-five years later
2013 – Fifty-six years later

Hopefully, you can sense and feel the same love and devotion many years later.

February 14, 2005 ~ Valentine's Day

Dear Bob,

I have been privileged to call you Sweetheart for forty-seven years. You are my one and only Sweetheart. Our life together has been exciting, happy, fulfilling and our home has been filled with love, peace, joy and faith.

You have set a wonderful example of a godly man for our sons and me. It is so rare to find a godly man today who has your sterling character. I thank you so much for being the example for our sons. I also thank you for being a man of God for me, for when my faith has wavered, yours has always been so strong.

For forty-five years I knew you were the most loving, caring husband in the world. But, the last few years you have really proved your love in so many ways. You have been right there with me through every pain and every heartache and we have cried together. You have been there when the news was good and we rejoiced together. I have been able to lean on you and your faith has remained strong. Thank you for always being there for me.

You are an incredible person, and a fabulous, wonderful husband and friend. You are my very best friend in all the world, and it is such a joy to share your life.

All my love, always,
Jan

Valentine's Day
2005

February 14, 2013 – Valentine's Day

This letter was in place of a Valentine's Day card, since Jan was at home recovering from amputation surgery.

My Darling Bob,

Today, you are having your second cataract surgery, and I am waiting for you and David King to return home. Today is also Valentine's Day. Remember our first Valentine's Day – an artist series and our picture was taken in Glide-Crawford Dorm? Our wedding was so beautiful and special! And to think – that was fifty-five years ago. At that time in my life, I didn't think I could ever love you more.

You have always been such a spiritual leader in our home. When the boys were born, you became such a terrific, fun father. You have always been such a loving, caring, godly husband and father, and grandfather – and great-grandfather!

The last ten years, since I have had health challenges, you have been right by my side. Today, I love you more than I could've dreamed as a young girl. I am more in love with you than I ever dreamed possible.

Thanks for being the kindest, most loving, most caring, most supportive, most devoted, most godly best friend a girl could ever have!

Thank you for loving me and constantly reminding me that God is in control of today and our future.

All my love, always,
Jan
2013

June 1, 2013
Our Fifty-sixth Anniversary

My Dearest Darling Bob,

There are no words to tell you how much I love you and how much you mean to me! When we married, I was so in love with you! Through the years, more and more love has been added. You have been my _best friend_ through all of life.

God blessed me so much when He led me to you! Our lives have been so much fun! We have been busy with a purpose. I have been blessed to be a part of your music ministry and of your "people ministry."

You have been the greatest husband through each aspect of our lives. You have been an awesome father, too! Life has been wonderful and you have made it so!

All my love, always,
Jan

Chapter Nine
Jan Fraumann's Celebration Service
(August 20, 2013)

http://tinyurl.com/BobbyFraumann

Bobby Fraumann – Grandson

Good Morning.........
First off, let me just say thank you, wow, for joining us in the celebration of my grandmother's life, a life well lived. From my family to all of you, thank you for being a part of it with us this afternoon. Thank you for joining in the celebration of my grandmother, Janice Marie Fraumann's life. It means so much that we can get to spend this afternoon with all of you.

My name is Bobby. I am the first and the only grandson of Bob and Jan Fraumann. I inherited all the good looks. That's my proclamation to the family. I'm claiming that. I also got her gene of fashion and style. I'm going to proclaim that one, too. I have a beautiful wife the Lord has blessed me with, a beautiful wife, the most beautiful wife in the whole world, in my mind. She's given me two beautiful offspring, Caydence and Michaela. I have a two and a half year old son and an almost one and a half year old daughter. In preparation for what I was going to say tonight I was asking my two kids, who were at the table with me, they saw dad writing down some stuff and they assumed that it was coloring time and they were going to get to color with dad. I asked them, Michaela, what would you say to Jan Jan if you could see her right now? She was too busy sucking on a fruit squeezer, which is awesome, and her eyes were in the back of her head, so I was like, this is not the time. So, I asked my son, Caydence, hey, what would you say to Jan Jan right now if you could talk to her? He looked and pondered for a minute, and it floored me and my wife what he said. He said "Happy Birthday Jan Jan." and for a minute and I was like, what? But it seemed so fitting that today we celebrate her birthday. One of the last words I ever got to tell my grandmother was "this is not goodbye, this is see you later. This is not death, this is life."

And, I was thinking about that as I was writing down with my family at the table with me, what I say, what verses stick out with me, and immediately the first verse that popped into my mind was Matthew 5:16 which says "in the same way, let your light shine before others that they may see your good deeds and that they would glorify your Father in heaven." My grandmother, Jan Fraumann, was the embodiment of that verse. I can attest to all the beautiful faces in this room. Her light shined bright and left a permanent mark, stain on every individual in here. I can look out, and I met so many people last night, and it was so overwhelming to hear story after story, and today as I look out into this congregation and the gathering assembled here today, I don't just see a face, and a face, and an individual, I see a story, and a story of a daughter, and a wife, and a mother, and a mother-in-law, and a grandmother, and a great-grandmother, and a friend, a beloved friend to all. Her life was her story. There was something about her that left its mark, its stain on our lives. We'll forever remember it. I've heard so many stories just in the last twenty-four hours that your grandmother was so gracious, she was so kind. Your grandmother was so loving. It hit me that in Galatians 5:22 you guys were all repeating the fruit of the Spirit – love, joy, peace, patience, kindness, goodness, gentleness, and self control, and that every story that I heard had that in common with it, that she was so sacrificial with her time.

I would just like to say real quick, because I've got a problem. I like to talk a lot, and I was telling my grandfather that the other night I didn't know what I was going to say, so I just went out and I started walking and talking, and it was drizzling, and I was speaking to myself, and it was twelve o'clock at night, and the neighborhood dogs were barking at me, and I got real loud and animated on what am I going to say and I looked down at my time and we were at forty-seven minutes. Bob Bob has only given me ten. So, I tried to barter some time from the family's other speeches, but they did not give me any. But, I want to cut it short and I want to keep it simple today, and keep it about Jan and glorifying her life and her light. My story is that, what I saw in my grandmother. No matter what situation she was in in her life, no matter what she was going to have to go through, she was always there for us. I remember as a kid she would take us to Wal-Mart. She would drop whatever it is that she was doing. When we were in our younger years, when we were little kids, she would say, "let's go to Wal-Mart, let's buy a toy." She would bring us back to the house, and not just throw us in the corner, she would play with us with that toy, or watch the Sound of Music, over and over and over and over again. And I'm scarred, but that was my grandmother, just truly, honestly, spending time. It wasn't fake, it wasn't phony, it was genuine, and it was real.

And then as I grew up, I saw it as it affected others, and whatever your story is, I encourage you and challenge you to tell it to someone else today. Whether you were in a prayer group or a small group and she spent time to pray with you. Or, you were in the hospital behind closed doors in treatment with her and she was gracious enough to say "hey, what's going on, let me pray for you." Or, if she was giving her testimony on this stage, and wanted to sit up here and pray with every person that needed prayer, even though it was uncomfortable after an amputation. She was sacrificing her time for everybody else, and what I want you guys to just think on, reflect on, was that it was not just my grandmother's love, it was not just her kindness or her gentleness, that it was the Father's love inside of her. It was the Father's kindness. It was the overflow of the Father's love inside her that was gushing out of her and affected everyone in her marketplace, everyone in her general vicinity. It was the Father's kindness that was the overflow.

Real quickly, we talked about the fruit of the Spirit and it's interesting that it was illustrated as a fruit, because fruit usually grows on trees. And, I thought about that for a long time. What does the tree have to do to grow any kind of fruit? Does it have any control over the weather? It needs sunlight. It needs rain. But, it can't control the sun and it cannot control the weather, but the tree needs those things in order to produce fruit in its life. And, the tree can only control one thing and that's how deep its roots grow in good soil. And I would say that about my grandmother, that her roots went deep in the Word, in her prayer life, in her relationship with Jesus. And as the result, you see the light that shined in her life, the fruit.

It reminds me of Peter when he walked on the water. I think everybody knows that story. Jesus sends his disciples into the boat and he says to go ahead of him across this lake. Peter is the head honcho, he's the fisherman, he's the captain of the boat, so he's been on it before, and he knows what to do. And, halfway through their journey somewhere they hit this storm. If anybody's been on a boat, I was in the Marine Corps for five years, I've been across the Atlantic, and there's some pretty big waves, and some pretty big storms. They are hard to ignore. They're hard to just put aside. I'm sure that Peter gets into survival mode. When a storm comes in your life, the first thing that we start to do is go into survival, take care of the boat, take care of myself, a selfish mentality, we've got to survive. But, here comes this beautiful Savior named Jesus. He walks out on the water and Peter sees Him. And, there was something in the eyes of Jesus that kept Peter fixated on him. It was intoxicating. It was the love of Jesus that Peter forgot the whole storm. He forgot the waves. He did something crazy. He stepped out of the boat. He abandoned himself. To me, that reminds me so much of my grandmother, that whether it was polio, she wasn't worried about herself, she stepped out of the boat and she started sacrificing for others. When she found out she had cancer, she was not in the boat, she was out of the boat dealing with other people, praying for other people. When she found out she had to have her leg amputated, she was in the hospital loving on other people.

When she found out she had two weeks to live, my last memory will always be when we went down there, I said "Jan Jan, we're not coming back. This is going to be the last time we see you". I got to tell her "this is not goodbye, this is see you later. And I said I want to pray for you". She said, "no, I want to pray for you." She prayed for me for fifteen minutes. And she prayed for my wife, my two children, and my sister, her husband, her three great grandchildren, Greg and Terri, Victoria, Sofia. It was about her praying for us, not about us praying for her in her last moments.

So today, as you think about Jan Fraumann and her life and her legacy, think about her light that was shining, and don't let her light fade with today's passing. I challenge each and every one of you to keep your eyes fixated on Jesus, and just like Peter, and just like my grandmother, when the storms come into your life, you'll find yourself not in the boat, but walking above the storms, above the waves. The storm of cancer, my grandmother fought with it, but she walked above it, and her light touched each and every person in this room.

Thank you so much again for coming and celebrating today with us. Truly, it is an honor to spend time with you. Thank you.

Chapter Ten
Jan Fraumann's Celebration Service
(August 20, 2013)

http://tinyurl.com/BrittanyFraumann

Brittany Fraumann Peterson – Granddaughter

My name is Brittany, and I'm Jan's granddaughter, and I did not inherit the genes of speaking that my grandfather, my grandmother, and my brother have. So if you're okay with it, I'm going to stick to my notes and we're all going to get through this together.

As I was thinking today about what I wanted to say about the life of my grandmother, the Proverbs 31 woman stood out to me. The woman that the scripture describes is quite an amazing woman. And, one that I feel that I will never quite measure up to, but that I will continue to strive to be like. In my opinion, my Jan Jan held all the qualities that the Proverbs 31 woman describes. I would like to share with you today just a few of the qualities that my Jan Jan possessed.

Proverbs 31:16 - She considers a field and buys it; from her own income she plants a vineyard.

When my brother and I were kids, we would go and spend the night at my Jan Jan's house. One of my favorite things we would do is go to work with her. She owned her own business and she operated it from her basement. When we spent the night, she would let us go to work with her. This was one of my favorite things to do. She always found little jobs for us to do. I loved watching my grandmother, how she would talk with customers over the phone and how she would handle all the everyday duties required of running a business. I realize now, that I own my own business, what all those "fun" days, how much they really impacted my life.

Proverbs 31:28 – She opens her mouth with wisdom, and loving instruction is on her tongue.

When my brother and I would stay at my Jan Jan's house, when we woke up in the morning she would teach me how to make one of my favorite breakfast dishes – Lost Bread. She always told me how the name of the dish was a French name, because it was a recipe from her French grandmother, Mama Julia, my great-great-grandmother. I grew up always knowing the wonderful stories of how my great-grandparents met, how they married, how many children they had, and what they did with their lives. This was very important to my grandmother because family was always her number one priority. She was and still is the heart of our family, and she worked very hard to spend her life to build a long and strong legacy and wonderful memories for our entire family to carry on to the next generations.

My Jan Jan always took time to influence my life. It wasn't just me, no she would do this to every single member of our family. My grandmother may have only given birth to sons, but she did an excellent job of being a loving mother and grandmother to all the girls that God put in her life to influence. I represent all the girls that she didn't give birth to herself, but that God gave to her to mentor. As I represent her daughters–in–law, her granddaughters, and her great-granddaughter, I feel confident that I can speak for all of us in saying that she was a wonderful example of what a true lady should be. She taught us all that a lady should always be hospitable, poised, graceful, elegant, kind, gentle, supportive, and of course, loving.

I can't count the number of times that she would spend giving me advice and encouragement about my life. I've learned some of my most valuable life lessons from my mother, who contributes learning them from my grandmother and has passed them down to me. My new mission, as I have just embarked into motherhood, is to now pick up and carry the legacy handed down to me from my grandmother.

There are countless times that I have heard my Jan Jan tell me how proud she is of me, and countless times that she has prayed blessings over my life, including in just her last few days. It wasn't because I am all that special, although she had a way of making me feel that I was. She did this to every single one in our family and so many others. Some of you are here, I'm sure. It was just simply her way of life. Speaking with wisdom and loving instruction was something that my grandmother did exceptionally well.

Proverbs 31:28 – Her children rise up and call her blessed, her husband also praises her.

I cannot think of a better example of this scripture than what you are seeing and hearing today. As her children, her grandchildren, and her husband all together rise up and call her blessed, and sing the praises of her life; loving and serving the Lord.

Proverbs 31:30 – Charm is deceitful and beauty is fleeting, but a woman who fears the Lord will be praised.

My grandmother was physically a very beautiful woman. Even as she lost her hair to all the chemotherapy, and as she lost her leg to the years of chemo and radiation that had deteriorated the bone in her leg, my Jan Jan's most attractive feature was the love that she had for the Lord that radiated through her. The way that she loved and served the Lord with her whole heart was the most beautiful feature that she possessed. I want to take this moment to celebrate my grandmother's life. I want to celebrate all the lives that she impacted for the Kingdom, and I want to tell you how thankful I am to have had her wonderful influence in my life.

In closing, I want to say that as I continue to miss her, I will rejoice over the fact that she is now dancing on her two legs in heaven and singing with lungs full of eternal life as she praises our sweet Lord face to face. Thank you.

Chapter Eleven
Jan Fraumann's Celebration Service
(August 20, 2013)

http://tinyurl.com/GregFraumann

My name is Greg, I'm Bob and Jan's youngest son, and I will have to kind of address what Bobby said earlier. He might claim the good looks and style for <u>his</u> generation, but I'm going to have to claim it for <u>my</u> generation, since I'm speaking before my brother. I wanted to share a song with you guys, because it's probably easier for me to sing than talk. Just reminds me of my mom and I wanted to share it with you.

Greg shares a solo, "Thank You" on YouTube

<u>Greg Fraumann – Son</u>

I did want to share a few thoughts with you. When I think of my mom, I think of a woman who was, as has been said before, selfless and generous, with a quiet strength, a true prayer warrior, a graceful, proper southern lady that had a great sense of humor, but don't tickle her or she'll smack you. But, most of all, I think of two things in particular, her unconditional love, "Do you know you are loved?" she would ask; she wanted to make sure that it wasn't just her words, but her actions as well. I've been told several times that the house I grew up in is like the Cleaver household, like *Leave it to Beaver*, and I'll have to tell you, it really was. I never heard my mom and dad argue, I never heard them raise their voice at each other. I'm sure they did, but it was behind closed doors, it wasn't in front of the kids. What a security that was for us as children to know that mom and dad were a team.

I remember, as a kid, mom would make the comment that I'm raising boys to be men. They'll have the weight of the world on their shoulders for the rest of their lives. So as boys, I want to take care of them. I remember things like on a cold winter day when I was in elementary school, or several days, she did this a lot, she would come in and wake me up for school and she'd have a pair of blue jeans for me to put on that she just pulled out of the dryer. She'd warm up my jeans for me. I'd stick my foot up in the air. She'd put a sock on my left foot. I'd stick the foot up to the right. It's just the funny memories that you go back to childhood and think of.

She was such an encourager. She believed in dad. She believed in Rick. She believed in myself, our whole family. She would always edify my dad. She wouldn't let anyone get away with criticizing him, whether it be anyone in the church, or friends, or my brother, myself. She always had his back. She would tell people, and now I'll tell you to always laugh at my dad's jokes. She would tell them "I've heard them a thousand times and I still laugh." So I want you to laugh, too. But, she always believed in us. She instilled in us that we could do anything, if we put our minds to it.

I remember as a kid, I was probably six years old, she asked me "What do you want to be when you grow up?" and I said, "Superman." And she said "Ok, That's interesting." And I remember asking," Can I be Superman?" She said, "Well, do you think you can?" I said "Well, I guess so." She said, "Well, if you think you can, you can." Now in her mind she wasn't thinking about wearing the blue tights and flying through the air. She had her own idea of what a Superman would be, and that was a lot like my dad. It is a lot like my dad, to be a man of God. Mom would always tell us that we're Fraumanns, we do things different. We would say, "So and so can do this, and so and so is doing that." She would say, "Well, they're not Fraumanns, are they? We're Fraumanns, we're different! We've got backbones. We swim upstream. We don't do what everybody else does. We stand up for what we believe in, and we do what's right, and that's who we are."

I was on the drive down from Ohio and I was talking to my girls. My oldest is twelve, Victoria, and my youngest is Sofia, she's seven. I was asking them, "Where is Mama Jan?" They said, "She's in heaven." I said, "You're right, she is in heaven." I asked, "Why is she in heaven? Is it because she was good person? Was it because she led Bible studies? Was it because she was a good wife, a good mother?" I reminded my kids, and they've heard this many times. But I reminded them that those are good characteristics, but it doesn't allow you into the gates of heaven. The Bible says in Romans 3:10 and 23, "As it is written, there is none righteous, no, not one. For all have sinned and fallen short of the glory of God".

I reminded my kids that God has a rulebook that we have to follow and the standard is so high that it's impossible to follow the Ten Commandments. I told them that if we sinned, just once, that we have to stand before a holy and a just God, and we have to pay the penalty for our sin, no matter how big or little. That penalty is separation from God for eternity. And I told my kids, "That means that Mama Jan can't go to heaven just because she was a good person. Being good doesn't get us to heaven." And as I am driving, I looked over my shoulder and I see Sofia, and her eyes were this big. I did remind them that someone paid that penalty, for Mama Jan and for us, by dying on the cross for her sins. And He's our Good Shepherd. Romans 5:8 says, "God commendeth His love towards us in that while we were yet sinners, Christ died for us."

When Mama Jan accepted Christ, as I was telling my kids, as her Savior and started to follow Him, at that moment the price was paid in full, and she received that gift of salvation. She received that ticket into the gates of heaven. Romans 6:23 says, "For the wages of sin is death, but the gift of God is eternal life through Jesus Christ our Lord." So my answer is there's only one way. And the Bible says in Romans 10:9, 10, 13, "If thou shalt confess with thy mouth the Lord Jesus and believe in thine heart that God hath raised Him from the dead, thou shalt be saved. For with a heart man believeth unto righteousness, and with thy mouth confession is made unto salvation. For whosoever shalt call upon the name of the Lord shall be saved." That's what my mom lived. That was her purpose, to share that message. Whether it be in a hospital, whether it be in the chemo clinic, whether it be the dry cleaners, whether it be IHOP, or the church, she would engage with people try to share that message with them. Since she's not here today to ask that question, I ask it of you, because that's what she lived her life for, was to share Christ, and she would ask, "Do you know Jesus as your personal Savior, and as your Lord?"

I remember in her last few days, mom would ask me to sing to her while we were with her. She asked me to sing *Victory in Jesus* and she is now experiencing that victory. My mom truly is a Proverbs 31 woman, and I am blessed and honored to be her son. I do rest in God's promises that those who accept Christ and follow Him will hear those words, "Well done, good and faithful servant." I know my mom heard those words, as her life was a testimony of her love and devotion to Christ. Today truly is a celebration, as we have assurance. Just like Bobby said, it's not a goodbye; it's a see you later. So, I love you mom.

I just want to bring up my two daughters real quick, Victoria and Sofia. They just wanted to share a couple of quick thoughts about Mama Jan.

http://tinyurl.com/Grandchildren-testimony

Sofia: "I love Mama Jan, but I miss her, but I know she's in a better place".

Victoria: "I just wanted to say that I love her as well, but she's not suffering anymore. What we say is that now she has a new body in heaven and she's doing cartwheels in heaven as well as singing and dancing."

Sofia, age 7

Victoria, age 12

Victoria, Greg, Terri and Sofia

Chapter Twelve
Jan Fraumann's Celebration Service
(August 20, 2013)

http://tinyurl.com/Son-Rick-testimony

Rick Fraumann – Son

Good afternoon. My name is Rick Fraumann, and I cannot believe that my brother and my own son shamelessly took this moment to try to pander shamelessly that they are the best looking of this offspring. I feel confident enough that I'm not going to go down that road. I do feel like this is the first funeral I've ever attended that needs an intermission at this point, but I don't think we're going to have one.

Well, there's so much I can say about my mom and there's so much that has been said. I heard so many stories last night and it was such a privilege. I just wanted to share with you a couple of characteristics and qualities that I think we all see in her. There's not a room full of people today because she taught us something in a Bible study, or because she spoke something that changed our life that was an "aha" moment. She did all these things. The reason that we're here is because she touched our heart. When someone touches your heart, you're never the same, and none of us will be the same. And, the things that she used to touch our heart were

94

obviously love. I always knew every day of my life that she loved my father. I always knew that she loved the Lord. There was never any question; I always knew that she loved me.

The best example that I can give you of this is when I was fifteen years old, and I was the oldest child, and one of my friends was sixteen, and he had his driver's license and we were going to go out and have a good time. It was the first time that I was going to be in a car with someone that wasn't an adult, and I'm sure if you're a parent, you've been though that. And that's a very trying situation. So, I was talking to my mom and I said we're going to go out. I don't even remember who it was or what we were going to do, but she said, "You can go on this one condition." She made me memorize this and she sat me down and she looked me in the eyes and she said, "I want you to tell him before you pull out of the driveway that he is carrying the most important cargo in the world, that you are more important than diamonds, rubies, emeralds, or millions of dollars. You are irreplaceable to me." I said okay. I had to practice it a couple times. She wouldn't let me out until I got it just right. So, I got in the car and we didn't do seatbelts back then, I don't think. So we just looked at each other, and I said, "Before we go, I've got to tell you something. It's very important." He said, "Okay, what is it?" "You can't back up, or put it in reverse, because she has made me promise that you are carrying the most important cargo in the world. I am more important than rubies, diamonds, emeralds, and all the millions of dollars in the world. When you carry me around today you need to be very cognizant of this fact." He looked at me like this was the stupidest thing he had ever heard in his life, and laughed, put it in reverse and we were gone. But, I never forgot it.

My mom was full of joy. She had joy. I always remember her smiling and laughing. We had a home full of laughter. We had a home full of smiles. She did laugh at my dad's jokes all the time. I remember on January the 10th of last year, the day that cancer ravaged the bone in her leg and it snapped. And, she was in horrifying pain and she sat down. They called 911 to come. While she was sitting there with my dad waiting for 911, she realized that it was her only great-grandson's,

Caydence, very first birthday. She got on the phone and she called him, and she sang "Happy Birthday" to him with a smile in her heart and a smile in her step. She wanted to be joyful. She wanted him to know that she had joy in the midst of her suffering. She sat up here back in January and said in her testimony that happiness is dependent on circumstances. Sometimes she had some pretty lousy circumstances like we all do. But, joy comes from the Lord.

She was a gentle person. She was very kind. I, like Greg, never remember her getting angry or raising her voice. I do remember her being very frustrated with my younger brother at times. But, he was very young and didn't know. She would lock herself in her room, she would come out later, and she would have a smile on her face. But, she did not ever raise her voice. She never yelled at me. She never yelled at my brother. She never slammed the door. She never went on a rant or rage. I'm sure she was angry and frustrated raising two teenage boys at different times in her life, a long span of her life, but she never showed that to us. She wanted her home to be one of peace. She told us that many times. She made an intentional effort for it to be filled with peace. When I think of her, I don't think of her running around that's hectic, but I think of her smiling, peaceful, laughing, loving. I do remember those days, and I don't think it was just your blue jeans, but I remember your underwear, your socks were all toasty warm because she didn't want Greg to be cold at the bus stop. I don't remember those days with me. I do remember them with Greg. I remember him smiling when he put his leg out, like that. She was thoughtful and caring and things of that nature, but you all have your own stories. Our stories are not different or better, we just have the microphone to share it with you.

What I want to say today is that those things that we saw in my mom's life, of all the characteristics that I want to take away from her life, there's one characteristic that rides above all of those things. That is when she was twelve years old, you all know her story if you spent any time with her, she lay in a hospital bed in isolation with polio. No one could see her except her mom or dad. They were in white. Everything was closed down. She couldn't see her friends. She was taken out of school. She lay there. Polio doesn't sound like much today, but it was a death sentence then. No one knew how it was transmitted. They didn't know what the cure was. They didn't know what it was, so they just put you away. It was sort of like leprosy in the New Testament times. As she lay there, a scared little girl at twelve years old looking up into the ceiling, and the darkness, she heard the doctor tell her mother and father, "She'll never walk. She'll never have children. She'll never lead a normal life." You know her story that she gave her life to the Lord that night and she said, "I hope you can give these things to me. I want these things. I will follow you all the days of my life."

The characteristic I admire the most about her is that she did follow the Lord all of the days of her life. There are a lot of us that start down that path and three days later we say, "This God thing is not working out," or three weeks later, or three months later, or three years later. We say that we tried that. It's not really there. That's a common story in our world today. But you know she didn't. She celebrated her seventy-fifth birthday right before she passed away, so for sixty-three years she hung on to Jesus and she wanted more of Him, and she got more of Him. He's faithful, and He gave her more of Him.

I've heard people say things, and I really appreciate what you're saying when you say it, because I know your heart, but I've heard people say, "She was an angel." I've heard people say that they broke the mold when they made your mother. I've heard people say, "There's nobody I've ever met like her." While I think most of that is true, I think if she was here she would say, "Don't put me on a pedestal. I'm not any different than you or anyone else." What was different about her? We all do have a mold and it's full of us. She spent her life pouring herself out of that mold and asking God to give her more. And He gave her more, and He filled her. And like Joe said, she kept it and she gave it away, and she kept doing that. I have a unique privilege of seeing fifty-two years of doing that. I saw what she did when I was two-years-old, and five years old, and eight years old. She had a stage. She was beautiful. She was stunning. She had a phenomenal voice. She had a platform. She had a spotlight in a large church. She had a spotlight in business. She spoke before thousands of people. I thought, "That's the way you influence people for God." It's that you're successful, and you have it together, and you have beauty, and you have wealth, and you have power, and you can show people that this is what God has done in your life, and they're going to want that. And you know, all that's true.

The last ten years of her life she didn't have that. It was all savagely taken away from her. She lost her hair, she lost her leg, she lost her voice, she lost the stage, she lost the spotlight, she doesn't speak in front of hundreds of people. But, the stories that I heard over and over, over these last two weeks, she impacted ten times more people in the last ten years of her life through her struggle. For a number of reasons, first of all, we can't all relate to that success, but we can all relate to struggle. We certainly can! And in that struggle, not only was she struggling then, she had a lifetime of living with the Lord. Like my son said, "She planted her roots firmly." And, as she poured her life out she begged for more of Him, and if you know her, she never was prideful about what she knew or she experienced, she wanted more. She wanted to learn more. She wanted to experience more. She wanted more of God's power, more of His love, more of His knowledge, more of everything. Not to hoard it up inside of her, but to give it away.

And, it reminds me of the fruits of the Spirit in Galatians, because all the things I mentioned to you, that are qualities and characteristics that I admire, and that we admire in my mother's life, Paul talks about them in Galatians five. He says the fruit of the Spirit is love, and it's joy, and it's peace, it's patience, and there's kindness, there is gentleness, there's thoughtfulness, and there's self control. All of those things that I said was that what my mother experienced. She would tell you today that they didn't come from herself. She would tell you that she tried to have them come from herself, just like we all do and it's not there. But what she did is, she spent sixty-three years chasing after Jesus fulfilling her promise to God. I hope you do these things in my life, but regardless, I'm going to follow you all the days of my life. The cry of a desperate twelve-year-old girl. The fruit of the Spirit, we plant a seed and we try to dig it up a week later and there's nothing.

We say, I guess, this seed stuff doesn't work. But after years and years and decades it developed into a vineyard in her life. Fruit, you can go grab it, and you pull it off the vine, and you taste it, and you bite into it, and it's sweet, and it's nourishing, and it gives you life. That's what she showed us. Taste and see that the Lord is good. All those qualities and characteristics that we admired in her were the fruit of the Holy Spirit being invested and grown through an entire lifetime. If there's something for us to take from that today, I would challenge us all, it certainly challenges me to hold on and be faithful and true. That's her side of the story.

Now, you know she has a partner in my dad, but before that she headed into a partnership, into a covenant with the Lord Jesus Christ, when she was twelve years old. She did everything in her power to fulfill what she promised Him. And you know what, she didn't walk the next day. She didn't walk a week later. She didn't walk a month later. I wonder if God is active in my life. I wonder if it meant anything. Her cousin Shirley talked to me last night. She was at the funeral home and she said, "You know I was there that day in church when your mother walked. I remember that." We looked through old scrapbooks and it said, the newspaper actually covered that then, that was a story that was newsworthy. I'm sure the Atlanta Journal would not cover it today, or the Marietta Daily Journal. But the Columbus paper covered it and said "New Legs on Easter." God, Jesus, who's extravagant, she found Him and I want to tell you that He is a HILARIOUS, EXTRAVAGANT giver. If you ever doubt that, think of the story of my mom.

As Greg pointed out, He paid the price for our sin. And, it's as like we owe a million dollars, to put it in a context that we understand, and we only have a hundred. And there's no way we can pay it. He sent His best. He sent His only Son, the best that He had that was more valuable to Him than rubies, diamonds, emeralds, and all of the money in the world. He gave the very best He had for my mother and for each one of us. That Son was beaten beyond recognition to pay the price for us, so that He overpaid. That's what He does. He didn't pay a million dollars and put into our account. He paid a hundred million dollars. So, if you ever doubt for one minute that "You don't understand, I'm not like Jan Fraumann, He could never forgive me." Not only did He pay for your sin, but there's a credit balance that far exceeds many times of what you could ever do. And, that's what He did in His partnership with my mom. She asked to walk, and she didn't walk right away, but you know, she walked. She walked many, many years. In the last ten years of her life, when she had eight surgeries and she had cancer ravaging a leg, and she had an amputation of a leg, it wasn't in the leg that had polio. It was in the other leg. He gave her not only another chance to walk, He extravagantly gave her more. When I was in the hospital room, when she woke up after she lost that leg, and she was learning to transition from one leg from a bed, to a wheel chair, and a wheelchair to a car, and she was struggling, that leg that had polio was the one that held her up for the last two years of her life and gave her strength.

She asked for a child, and I think that's why she loved me so much. It was nothing I did, I did nothing. But, I was the first part, and Greg was the next part of the fulfillment of her longing and her dream and her prayer, to please give me children. And on January second of this year, when she was in Austin at our house, Nate and Brittany birthed her third great-grandchild, Jonathan Robert. She was there in the hospital and got to hold him about an hour afterwards. Caydence and Michaela were there, and all three of her great-grandchildren were there, and I remember as she held Michaela, that little girl, she just wept with tears of joy. I said, "Mom, what's wrong?" She said, "I can't explain it. There are no words. I cannot describe to you, I cannot tell you of the joy that I have. I never thought I would see this moment, to see this far. I hoped for children, and I thought about grandchildren, but I never thought God would be so gracious and so merciful, and so awesome to let me see this in my life. And He did." I think He was just laughing with tears of joy, because she bargained for something and He gave her so, so, much more!

The last thing I'll tell you, and I'm sorry she prayed for Greg and I to have tender hearts, so I can't help it, she prayed for this. The last thing that she prayed for and hoped for was a normal life. I've been to a lot of funerals and usually there are five people there, there's not a full house, standing room only at someone's funeral. She had anything but a normal life. God gave her an extraordinary life, a life filled with meaning and purpose, and power, and difference! She touched people's lives and she made a difference in their lives and I've heard many of the stories. She never had a normal life because He is so big and He is so powerful, and He is so good, and He is so extravagant that she didn't realize. You don't realize it in a day, and you don't realize it in a year. You only realize it when you look back and you have a chance to reflect.

She would tell me to tell you today she wasn't anything unique or special. She was a little girl that was desperate for God, and she held on to Him, and was faithful all the days of her life. She could not believe how much He loved her and how extravagant His love and His blessings were to her. I know that she is with Him. She's looking into His face, and she is overcome because she thought that she made a great, hard bargain when she was a little girl and she had no idea what she was getting into.

Mom, as you look into the face of Jesus, and you're filled with His joy, we all know and we're all here to tell you that you were very loved and that we love you so much. Thank you.

Nate, Brittany, Jonathan Peterson,
Laura, Rick Fraumann,
Cadence, Sabrina, Bobby, Michalea Fraumann

101

Chapter Thirteen
Jan Fraumann's Celebration Service
(August 20, 2013)

http://tinyurl.com/Husband-Bob-testimony

Bob Fraumann – Husband

Sorry, this is a long celebration, but I planned it and you can blame me later.

I only had one crack at this to share with you the life of my Sweetie, and you see it in my family. I want to settle this issue about handsomeness – you see where it started guys? I want to thank you for coming and honoring this saint that I lived with, my wife, Jan. I know she's not here. She's with Jesus. You're about to hear her sing in just a few minutes, like you've never heard anybody sing. We're all here to celebrate the life of this saint. I should know. I lived with her for fifty-six years, twenty-four seven. What you've experienced of my Sweetie would be a few hours here and there, or wherever it may be, but I lived with her that long. Fifty-six out of fifty-six years of happy marriage is pretty good. THANKS BE TO GOD!

The hour she went to be with her Lord was a week ago last night. A rainbow appeared! Do you remember that? Laurie was rushing over to our home to be with me and she took a picture of that. It's like a statement of saying, "Hey, Bob she's here!"

We have no regrets, just memories. The reason for that is we planned it that way, from day one. We put God first in our marriage, and it was one hundred percent / one hundred percent. I did whatever had to be done, no matter what it was. She did whatever had to be done. It wasn't a fifty/fifty. We prayed before our dates. We prayed during our dates. We even prayed after our dates. That's a pretty good rule to date by, isn't it, huh? When we married, we prayed for both of these boys when they were in the womb; like Rick said, number one, that they would have a tender heart sensitive to God. You can see that. But number two, we prayed that they would be good looking, and they are. Thirdly we prayed for the girl that they would marry and their children. Now, our children and grandchildren have called us so many times, because they are at a distance, and prayed for my Sweetie on the phone, even as young as four years of age, that God would be with her and help her.

So, I am happy to say, as you've already witnessed today, that my family knows Jesus Christ in their heart as Lord and Savior. I'm not bragging about that. We planned it that way, from day one. Jan was really the prayer warrior in our lives! I've learned so much from her. Whatever I am today, I can thank her for that. She backed me a hundred percent in my church music for over fifty years, and the businesses that we owned, as well. Yes, she would fuss at you if you didn't laugh at my jokes.

I always liked prestige tags and had different names on them. One time we had two tags, and I was the "King" and she was the "Queen." That was on our cars. I believe if you treat your wife like a queen, she'll treat you like a king. The only problem I had with that was when I was driving her car. I got some interesting looks!!!

We had some rules in our home, and it's already been alluded to, a home of peace and happiness. We blessed our home. We've had, I can't begin to tell you, thousands and thousands and thousands of people come through our home because of church and business. We prayed for every one of you, that you would be blessed. We prayed for blessings upon our physical home. We prayed that when you would come into our home, that you would feel the Holy Spirit and the warmth and the happiness there. I hope you did.

Divorce, we never even thought of. Like Rick said, yelling, cussing, slamming doors, temper tantrums, that just didn't happen. We prayed for both of our boys when they became Christians. Both of them were around twelve. We had the honor and the privilege of praying for them, in our home, on our knees, when they accepted Christ into their life.

Jan always said that the wife in the home is either a <u>thermostat</u> or a <u>thermometer</u>. If the wife is a thermometer, she's up and down, and up and down, and up and down, happy and sad, whatever the thing may be. But, a wife really needs to be the thermostat, because a thermostat controls the atmosphere of the home. I'm reminded of the guy that saw a lady wearing her wedding ring on her index finger. He said, "Is that your wedding ring on your index finger?" She said, "Yeah." He said, "Well, it's on the wrong finger." She said, "I married the wrong guy." Thank you, I need some humor right now for survival.

Let me throw this at you. Christianity is not a religion. If we're just going to come here and sit in church here and do our little thing week to week, or whatever it is, it's not a religion. Christianity, is an experience, a personal relationship with Jesus Christ. So, coming to church and just sitting here every Sunday doesn't make you a Christian any more than sitting in a chicken coop makes you a chicken.

Jan really studied. It's been said so many times today that she studied; she was a student of the Bible with passion. She took every course she could find on how to be a better wife, on how to be a better mother, how to be a better homemaker. She studied the blessing, which came out of the Jewish tradition in the Old Testament. She loved that. I was blessed every day by my mother before I went to school, that I would have a good day and get along with my teachers, not have an accident, or whatever. I thought that was normal. I found out that it isn't. She loved to do that. She's taught many of you those courses. We started three Bible studies here and many of those are continuing.

Let me ask you this personal question. How many of you all have been personally touched by my Sweetie, or challenged, or prayed for, or counseled with, or blessed, or had some personal encounter that touched you to help you see Jesus in a better way, would you raise your hand? Wow!!!

On her death bed, Bobby told you about this, she brought in every member of the family, laboriously trying to breathe, and she personalized every prayer for many, many minutes on every one of them. It's something I've never experienced before. Her cousin by marriage is Derric Johnson, who has been the Music Coordinator for Disney for many, many years. I called and told him the situation with Jan. He married into the family about ten years before I did, and so he knew her growing up. Two hours later his wife called me in the "Voices of Liberty" at the American Pavilion in Disney at Epcot. His wife called and said "Bob, would it be okay if we sang 'Happy Birthday' to Jan?" She had a Happy Birthday from Disney in eight-part acapella harmony. What a blessing!

We've had an incredible life together. It's been happy. It's been spiritual. She's been a passionate lady to live with. Lots of fun in our life together. We took two years off many, many years before I came to Mt. Zion. We just traveled. We hit twenty-four islands in twenty-four months. We spent a week or two out on the road and just had a blast. I remember one time Greg said, "Don't you want me to go with you? I could keep you company." I said, "We can handle it, Greg. We can handle it. We can handle it. We like each other."

She never complained. The DVD that was made of Jan sitting right here back in January, if you haven't seen it, you need to. Ken Grimme made that for us, and I have many of them right now. I will have, after the service today, if you'd like to see what she said that will touch your life. You can Google it. It has a crazy title she came up with, "A

One-Legged Great-Grandmother Has A Personal Encounter With God And The devil." She did.

Jan walked this aisle after some of those surgeries. She had to learn how to walk again. This was her therapy place. I can remember her going pew by pew by pew. The next day we'd add another pew. She was always looking at this beautiful window of Jesus holding the lamb. That was her inspiration. I was her cheerleader. "Come on, you can do it!" One more pew, one more yard. We measured it off in yards. It was just such a joy, just to cheer her on and have her therapy right here where you're sitting.

We've intentionally strived to have an incredible legacy and I see that happening. Nothing would thrill Jan any more than to see you develop a legacy for your family. If you do that, start today, and I want you to tell me about it.

Our marriage was over fifty-six years and it's been a good trip. It's really been about as long as I can remember that we've been married.

Jan had a list of qualifications when she dated people. Some of you have heard this. I knew she had a list after I started dating her, but I didn't know the details of that list. She had thirty line items. Every time she would have a date, she would come in and check it off. We were eighteen when we got married, and she had already been proposed to three times. I was lucky I even got in. But, if I'd have seen that list before we were married, I'd have just kept walking. Just kept walking – no way! But, I have that list girls, on my iPhone, if you want to see it, and guys, too. You need to have a list before you decide who you are going to marry, because this whole thing started that you saw today, when I asked her for a date, and all this had come out of that date. I just asked the right lady at the right time!

I only had two qualifications. Some have heard this. I believe if you're walking and living in God's will that He has your life planned for you. That's plan A! Who you're going to marry, and what your career's going to be. If you just live in the center of God's will, He's going to make it a great trip for you. I can remember as a teenager saying, "Oh God, I know you've got somebody out there picked for me, please don't let her be ugly." I don't want to have to wake up in the morning and look over there and say, "Oh no." I meant that as serious as a heartbeat. I said, "I want a good-looking chick." But, I said I was raised by a godly mother, and I also wanted her to be godly. It's almost like an oxymoron, isn't it? Good looking chick, and godly? It worked for me. I just called her my "sexy saint"!!!

We prayed for Jan's healing for ten years. We just couldn't figure out why God didn't heal her. You heard the story about her being healed from polio. Jan's sister, ten years ago, died with the same thing, the same thing that Jan had. I remember when Tom Pilgrim came and prayed with us, he comforted Jan by saying, "Jan, we've been praying for your sister for so long, but she's had the ultimate healing. She's in heaven with Jesus. She's had the ultimate healing." My mother-in-law sitting right here, she's ninety-four. She's lost three husbands and three children. I just don't see how she does it. I want to thank you, Mama Mae, for Janice. Thank you for taking care of her that year when she was recovering from polio. Thank you, and I love you dearly.

I miss her greatly. I'm having to embark on a whole new life. I'm trying to already adjust to that. I need your help. Invite me over for dinner, just stick an extra plate on the table, okay? That's a whole lot better than bringing me a whole bunch of food. Some of you are concerned about how much I'm going to eat or whatever, yeah, I'm going to eat. I just don't like to eat alone. I'm counting on you to do that.

You're going to hear her sing in just a few minutes. We're going to show a PowerPoint of her life. The first song she's going to sing is called "Prayer." It's one of the most beautiful songs I've ever heard. She's going to also sing "It Took a Miracle." When she would give her testimony about her healing of polio, she would always sing this song at the very end. I can't tell you how many people were won to Christ through her testimony and her singing. It's been a long time since I've heard her be able to sing. My son, Rick, recorded her right here, when

107

I was doing my CD ten or twelve years ago. He said, "Mom, why don't you come over here and sing a couple songs?" She said, "I'm not warmed up." He said, "Come on, just come over and sing." You're going to hear that. Not too many people sing at their funeral, but I'll tell you, she will blow your socks off. She was such a gorgeous lady, and wife with a voice that she has. I'm just looking forward to seeing it again.

Jan ran the race. She finished strong, and she's already heard the Lord say, "Well done, good and faithful servant, enter thou into the joy of your Lord. Welcome home Jan." So, she's singing in heaven right now and she's going to sing for you right now.

TO GOD BE THE GLORY.

http://tinyurl.com/JanSinging

Jan, age 2

Jan, age 3

Jan, age 18

"Royal Heirs Trio" 1954-57
Katie, Jan, Vera, Mary Helen (pianist)

Valentine's Day, 1956
This is the night I asked Jan to "Go Steady".
That's why she is so happy!

Jan and Bob, 1956
(the first time Jan ever saw snow)

Bob and Jan, 1956

Jan, 1957

Bob and Jan, 1957

Bob and Jan, 1957

Janice Fraumann

Jan, June 1, 1957

Our Wedding, June 1, 1957

Just Married, June 2, 1957

Easter, 1958

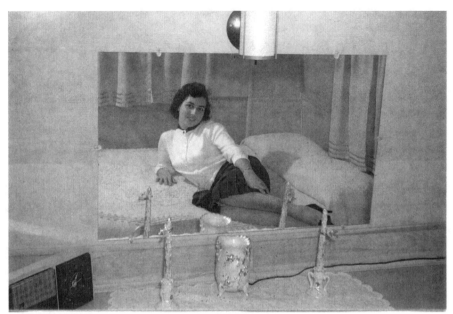

Jan, 1959

Bob and Jan, 1960

Our Family, 1980
Bob, Jan, Rick, Greg

Bob and Jan, 1980

Bob and Jan, 1985

Jan and Bob, 1985

Jan, 1986

Jan, 1987

Jan, 1988

Janice Fraumann

Jan, 1988

Jan hand-made Rick and Greg "life quilts" representing
their lives from birth to wedding for Christmas 2010

Personal postage stamp, 2012

Jan swimming in June, 2013,
two months before passing away,
with her three men, Bob, Rick, Greg

Chapter Fourteen
Remembrances
From
Family and Friends

Friends

When I think of friendship,
I think of you.
Thank you for being my friend.

A friend loves at all times.
The heartfelt counsel of a friend
is as sweet as perfume and incense.
If one falls down,
his friend can help him up.
But pity the one who falls
and has no one to help him up.
Dear friend, I am praying
that all is well with you
and that your body is as healthy
as I know your soul is.

Proverbs 17:17 NIV Proverbs 27:9 NLT
Ecclesiastes 4:10 NIV 3 John 1:2 NLT

Used by permission "Precious Word"

Jan, was undoubtedly, a special gift from God to all of us. Interestingly, each of us can be that special gift to our family and others.

Jan is that example.

My prayer, for you, is that you will:

- Accept Christ in your life
- Find a deeper relationship with Him
- Be that special person for God and others
- Establish a legacy for your family
- Initiate these blessings in your family

If, so, please let me know at bob@bobfraumann.com.

Hopefully, this biography will have an eternal impact on your life!!!

There is an intertwining, beautiful thread that runs through all these many remembrances of Jan!

- Can you find it?
- Do you feel it?

God bless,

Bob

Many family and friends have expressed their relationship with Jan and how she impacted their lives. Following are these letters.

In putting some of my thoughts on paper about my cousin, Jan, I feel I can't get across to you who she was. Words fail me. When I was young, we lived in Columbus, Georgia, and her family did, also. My father was her mother's brother. I am six years younger than Jan. First of all, let me say, Janice was beautiful! All of the boys were in love with her. I went to her house often to play with her younger sister, Bonnie. One time during my visit, Jan washed my hair with Prell shampoo, such happy memories of childhood. Janice contracted polio, a catastrophic disease, when she was about twelve years of age. There was no vaccine or treatment at that time, and there was obviously great concern. My parents and I went to see her at her home. She was in her bedroom lying on a raised platform with a pad on top. The platform was hard and gave her support. She was confined to bed, but did exercises to help strengthen her leg. I remember her showing me how she could lie down on her stomach, curl her legs up and touch the top of her head. She obeyed doctor's orders, she wasn't able to go out with her friends, or be involved in their activities. During this time, Janice gave her heart to God. Jan was <u>WISE</u>.

Over time, Janice recovered, but was left with some weakness in one leg. On Easter Sunday, a year or so after contracting polio, Janice was able to come to church. After Sunday school, my parents and I went outside to the front of the church. We waited for Janice to come out and walk down the front steps. She was dressed for Easter and looked beautiful! The local paper had reporters and photographers there to record her MIRACLE, for truly it was a miracle! All the cousins were so excited! We had a celebrity in our family! Her story and picture made the front page of the paper.

Janice was <u>WISE</u> – she had given her heart to God and placed her life in His hands. She didn't necessarily have family as wise, for she had insight most people just do not have. I believe, like Mary the mother of Jesus, Janice pondered things and kept them in her heart. It wasn't that her life was completely easy in every way, for it was very hard in many ways. Janice was gifted and greatly accomplished as society rates success, but she was much, much more. She was spiritually successful. God was in everything she did. She took nothing for granted. She prayed about everything. I'm afraid I took many things for granted. Janice was <u>WISE.</u> Oh, to be wise in God's eyes. She was unique! One of a kind! No other like her!

After Janice lost her leg, I went to visit her in rehab at Manor Care. She told me of her ministering to and praying with several patients who were devastated because of their situation. Janice was <u>WISE.</u> Her rehab wasn't easy.

We talked about a song we sing in church, "God's promises are never known to fail, no cloud of darkness over them shall prevail. They are builded sure and strong for the conflict with the wrong, God's promises are never known to fail."

At times, clouds may have obscured her view, but Janice clung to those promises. She knew that God's promises had never failed her, and never would.

Janice was <u>WISE</u>!!! What a fantastic family you have! What an example to follow! I hear your wonderful laughter and your sweet smile! I cherish the times we had together! What a privilege to be your cousin! <u>I love you, Janice, for always</u>!

Shirley Prince Smith
Cousin

There are so many wonderful things to be said about Jan. She had a tremendous impact on my life. She modeled for me the example of a godly woman, wife, mother, and grandmother. I am thankful that she was the mother that she was, and how she raised my husband. I feel blessed that she never looked at me like a daughter-in-law, but she looked at me like her very own daughter, and loved me that way. No matter what was going on, she always had a way of setting the atmosphere for those around her to be peaceful and positive, even when she was very sick. She was a wonderful role model for me and for our family. I will always be thankful to her for that.

She always led by example. She was an amazing leader and teacher. She led in her family, in her ministry, and in her business. She was a disciple of Jesus Christ. She knew the importance of praying for her family. She prayed diligently for her husband, her children, her grandchildren, and the rest of her family.

She was full of the love of the Lord. She loved her family and she loved others. She was a servant. She never took from others, but she was always a giver.

She was truly a gift to me and to our family. She was the heart of our family. I loved her dearly, and I will miss her every day until the Lord reunites us.

Laura Fraumann, Rick's wife

Thank you for praying for me for over forty-four years. You prayed for Greg's wife years before I was even born. My life shows those hundreds of prayers that were lifted up on my behalf. Greg is my treasure, and an amazing gift. Thank you for raising a son who loves the Lord above all else, and leads his family with such love and care. We miss you, but rejoice you are with Jesus. I will see you again one day.

I love you,

Terri Fraumann, Greg's wife

Jan came into my life with a song. I asked her to sing at my wedding when I married her brother, Ron. She blessed us with The Lord's Prayer that day. It was so beautiful! We had not known each other before, but we had an instant bond. Jan was always easy for me to talk and laugh with. I think with my being the same age as her younger sister, Bonnie, that she extended that sisterly grace to me. I can't think of a time that she was too busy to give her love and advice and prayers to me and my family. Jan did not have a selfish bone in her body. Whenever I would ask her to pray about something that was concerning to me, I knew that she took it to heart, and that she took it to God.

Jan was a real southern lady, and had a visible grace that shined like a bright light. She truly lived her life serving God and anyone who needed her. She was a wonderful wife and mother, and her family was central to her life. She was remarkable in how she accepted polio at age twelve, a severe burn to her body in 1970, and finally several bouts with cancer and the loss of her leg without complaint the last years of her life.

I don't think I shall ever know anyone like Janice Marie Fraumann again. She set a very high bar for all who knew and loved her and I shall always miss her.

With love,
Polly Barnes
Sister-In-Law

As a cousin of Jan's and six years younger, she had an unspoken impact on my life. Without realizing it, I followed her to Asbury (College) University, being the first on my father's side to go to college. I was so impressed with her beauty and love of life. Her laugh was one of the things that I will always remember. She laughed with you and never at you.

She was just beginning her wedding catering and bridal coordinating business, when my wedding came along in 1966 and she planned it all. Our families were very interwoven in our younger years. We shared the same experiences with our wonderful grandparents in the summers. I called her many times for advice within my church. I will truly miss her. Can't wait to see her in Heaven!!!

Dee Hilton
Cousin

Jan came into my life during the first years of my church music ministry in Montgomery, Alabama.   She was just beginning her educational career at Asbury (College) University in Wilmore, Kentucky… and because of a fortunate family connection, she was often in town visiting us from her home in Columbus, Georgia. I have often thought of my first recollections of this amazing young woman.

She was outrageously beautiful, charming and well mannered, mentally edging toward brilliance, all the while possessing a deep and abiding faith in the Lord Jesus Christ.   Couple that with outstanding singing ability and stunning stage presence… and you have a complete package.

I had her sing every time she was in town… and she never failed to point the audience in the right direction. All she needed was a great husband to partner with… and she happily found the exact right one in Bob. I have been thrilled to know him as well as Jan… and it has been pure joy through all these intervening years to call them friends.

Derric Johnson
Cousin, Composer, and Arranger

Janice Fraumann

Aunt Jan was such an amazing woman. I can honestly say that I've never know anyone quite like her. No matter what extreme pain and suffering she was experiencing, she would counsel others in need. She seemed to always know just how to lift people up when they were going through their own struggles. She had a special connection with God.

Her faith was stronger than anyone that I've ever known, and she displayed it with such grace and dignity, just as she lived her life. She was full of joy, embraced life and lived it to the fullest. Despite the physical hardships that came her way, she always thanked God, and celebrated all that He had given to her.

I could never truly express how much her sweet spirit influenced my life. I thank God for allowing me the opportunity to know her, learn from her, and love her.

Julie LaFond
Niece

Remembering Jan brings real joy as I remember our college years at Asbury (College) University. Our Lord Jesus brought Jan and Kathleen (Stephens) Hodges and me together to form a girls trio (The Royal Heirs) to sing and testify for our Lord and Savior Jesus Christ.

It was our joy and privilege to sing and give praise and testimony in youth groups and worship services from the mountains in Eastern Kentucky to Springfield, Illinois, as well as in our chapel services at college. We were very blessed to have our gifted pianist, Mary Helen (Tanquary) Morris to accompany our singing.

Jan was a wonderful Christian friend and such a very special "sister in Christ." I loved her as a very special friend. Singing together in our trio was such an answer to prayer. Every person that God brought into my life was God's plan at work. Jan was one very special sister in Christ. Her singing the middle part of the trio was not easy. I sang soprano which was quite easy.

Vera (Johnson) Dean
College Friend

The freshman girls who lived in Glide-Crawford Dorm at Asbury (College) University were a special "lot" – and Jan (Brown) Fraumann was one of them. She had a young girl look – dimples, full skirts, a beautiful figure and face. We all knew she had polio as a child, (and carried a slight limp with her as a result), but it didn't create a problem for her. All of us stayed in the same general area of Glide-Crawford Dorm, for the three years when we were all single.

I never knew Janice to show anger; I never knew her to act unhappy. We enjoyed singing together and often spent time in crowded cars to – or from – a concert we had prepared. Janice, Vera (Johnson) Dean, and I made up "The Royal Heirs" – a trio that sang in churches and auditoriums from Kentucky to Indiana and Illinois. Mary Helen (Tanquary) Morris was our accompanist.

When Don and I eloped, but had a formal church wedding, Bob and Jan provided the music.

Katie (Stephens) Hodges
College Friend

When I hear the name Jan Fraumann, a smile immediately comes to my mind. My thoughts take me back to 1954 when I arrived at Asbury (College) University. Of course I knew her then as Janice Brown – the cute "Georgia Peach" with beautiful brown eyes, and a smile that caught the attention of not only the guys, but all of us.

Somehow (the Lord planned it) we formed a trio called "The Royal Heirs." I accompanied the three girls – Katie, Vera, and Janice. Our backgrounds were as different as where we came from – Illinois, Ohio, West Virginia, and Georgia, but immediately our hearts were blended and we knew we had a common goal – to share His love through music. Those were wonderful days, and the Lord blessed us as we used music to bless others.

I thank God for the sweet memories of Jan! Heaven has to be a better place with her presence. It brings a smile to my face as I think of her there – singing and praising our wonderful Lord – yes, that's our sweet "Georgia Peach."

Mary Helen (Tanquary) Morris
College Friend

The "Royal Heirs"
(1954-1957)

Vera, Jan, Katie
Mary Helen (pianist)

The "girl" from Columbus, Georgia arrived in Kentucky at Asbury (College) University with our Cahok (freshman) class in September, 1954. I remember those "dreamy" eyes, the soft-spoken lady who came from a loving and caring family. Jan became my friend because she truly cared. Her lovely contralto voice inspired us with her deep appreciation and practice of her faith. Jan's singing in a ladies trio (The Royal Heirs) and my accompanying The Messengers Quartet kept us in the spirit of musical leadership in His kingdom. And when in the middle of our college years she chose Bob as her life-mate (or did He choose her?), we continued our journey through musical ministries as life-long friends.

Our family visits and travels as Jan and Bob raised their sons, and we raised our daughters, are some of our fondest memories. Her outstanding leadership and lectures to large groups of business acquaintances always maintained the depth of her personal faith. She led by action, patience, persistence, and love. Her personal dedication, in the words of her sons and lifetime companion, spoken at her "home going" service recorded earlier in this book(chapters nine, ten, eleven, twelve and thirteen) reminds me of why Jan left an indelible imprint on all of us. Thank you, Jan, as you rest in the arms of Jesus.

Merlin E. Johnson
College Friend

God's Blessed Angel

Jan and I were college classmates and dorm mates. She was always kind, sweet and smiling, the same temperament every day.

I remember catching the Lexington, Kentucky bus to go shopping with Jan and Pat (Kingsbury) Peters one year a couple of weeks before Easter. We went to one of the department stores. We tried on outfits (dresses, gloves, hats, shoes and jewelry). I think Jan was the only one going back to Asbury with a complete Easter outfit. What fun giggling and laughing that day.

Jan was a true loyal and genuine friend, a student of prayer. When Jan said she would pray for me and my problems, I knew I could depend on her going to the throne of God on my behalf. She was a woman of God's own heart, a beautiful lady inside as well as outside.

Jan is now singing alto in the heavenly choir. I love and miss her.

Phyllis (Weiss) Lowery
College Friend

From the first time I encountered Jan on the campus of Asbury (College) University until the last time I was privileged to enjoy her beautiful presence in her delightful home in Marietta, Georgia, I was deeply impressed with her southern charm and obvious beauty. Her beauty was not just external, but was manifested from her inmost being. Her beauty was spiritual as well as physical. Her beauty was enhanced by her exquisite singing voice.

When she fell in love with a handsome musician named Bob and they became husband and wife, I had no doubt that they would make beautiful music together that would enhance and bless the lives of untold numbers of people. And, that is certainly what happened to the glory of God and the pleasure of all who have known them. Gaynelle and I are eternally grateful that Jan and Bob have touched our lives in such wonderful ways across the years.

Doug and Gaynelle Newton
College Friends

Janice Fraumann was a vivacious, enthusiastic lady who was always the same – a friend to all. She was a delight and joy to be around and to fellowship with. She was an upbeat person, totally committed to God, who lived a full and rich Christian life.

Jan was never intimidated by physical challenges her entire life. Her victorious spirit gave her peace and fulfillment to the end.

Her precious influence will last through the future years reflected in those who loved her so much.

She was a testimony of grace.

Jerry and Karla Dooling
College Friends

Janice Fraumann

Janice and I met at Asbury (College) University in 1955. We became roommates and friends. We had many fun times together, laughing and just enjoying each other. We loved shopping and attending special services together. Janice will always be an inspiration to me, because of her loving ways.

Patricia Kingsbury Peters
College Friend

God's Blessed Angel

Janice Brown Fraumann, affectionately known as Mrs. Fraumann or Mama Jan, was the most beautiful person I have met. She never complained, though she may have been justified if she ever would. I met Jan in the infusion center of Emory University Hospital's Midtown Campus, Atlanta, Georgia. Some years ago she presented to the infusion center, not knowing what to expect and full of questions. When I looked into her soft brown eyes, I gave her my name and told her what I was going to do for her that day. There was a connection there I could not explain. She began to speak with her calm and gentle voice to ask questions about her treatment. At the end of her visit, I knew she was an angel sent by God to encourage me. I knew she was someone special!

When she would come into the facility, she would ask for me and call me her private nurse. I felt proud to be her nurse. We would talk about her family, and with what she explained, I knew she was loved by anyone she met. In fact, I do not believe she ever met a stranger. I loved Jan dearly. We would talk, laugh, cry, and sometimes share God's Word or a prayer. There were days when I did not feel my best, and then she would come in and perk me up.

I enjoyed our talks, but I did not know her full history until the year before she transitioned home to be with the Lord. I have since wondered if I would have been the same, but knowing what I know about Jan, she would not allow anyone to feel sorrow or pity for her. She was bubbly most days. When she was not, those were the days we both were lifted up in spirit. I could always be assured she was encouraging someone, even when she was not at her best.

I remember the day she had her leg removed. I walked into the hospital room and she was discussing marriage with a young surgeon. She was explaining to him that he should save himself for his wife.

I will tell you one thing, she was a beautiful lady, and a lady indeed. At her wake, I was able to capture pictures of her I had never seen. I had to ask myself if I recognized her from a movie or a television program. I will truly miss her; the smiles, the hugs, and those beautiful soft brown eyes, the love we shared between sisters, and her very presence. I will always remember Janice Brown Fraumann, because she touched my life in a special way.

Denise Gates-Baker
Nurse

Being one of Jan's doctors was easy for me. We became friends almost immediately. She was always so kind and pleasant. As our doctor-patient relationship grew, I discovered a woman that met the final challenge of hemipelvectomy supercharged by her faith in God, our Father, and her loving husband. I have not witnessed many patients enduring this metastatic cancer the manner in which Jan had done.

Only a few of us ever seem to get our priorities in the right order. Knowing Jan has allowed me to help minister to others when terminal illness makes them ungrateful, angry, or depressed. As the many cancer challenges faced her after time, I never saw a moment where her inner strength was dampened. Now I know why – Jan was loved by God, her dear husband, Bob, and her family.

Dr. Charles R. Haendel
Doctor

I was blessed to meet the Fraumann's in February, 2013 as Jan's caregiver. Mr. and Mrs. Fraumann truly are a blessed, spirit-filled couple. The term equally yoked is an understatement. The Fraumann's name should appear in Webster's dictionary – "equally yoked."

Mrs. Fraumann was surely "God's Angel On Earth." Definitely a "virtuous" woman. Proverbs 31 one hundred percent describes Mrs. Fraumann. As a couple, I never heard a harsh word or irate tone of voice with them. The Fraumanns are a model couple for everyone, especially Christians.

The Fraumann household is one of PEACE. They always had a loving welcome and smiles for me. The Fraumanns always displayed affection towards one another holding hands.

Mr. Fraumann had a signature "whistle" when he entered the home to let her know it was him and not a stranger. Bob and Jan's Legacy has been established for generations in the Fraumann family.

Mrs. Fraumann made sure others in her presence (church members, neighbors, friends) were kind to me. When her health started to decline and the Fraumanns became more dependent on church members and friends to provide meals and other services, she asked me in her soft spoken voice "Are they being nice to you?" I always replied, "Yes, they are." When I would leave for the evening she would say, "I love you, darlin." Such a "southern belle."

The last month of Mrs. Fraumann's life – the entire Fraumann family from Texas and Ohio (sixteen) came into town to comfort her. I have never in my life seen such love from a family like I did amongst the entire Fraumann clan. It was amazing!

Being in the presence of Mr. and Mrs. Fraumann has influenced me to follow their legacy for my family – to be a loving, spirit filled, Christ centered family, and to establish a legacy for my family.

146

The last week of Mrs. Fraumann's life she prayed for <u>all</u> of her family members: sons, daughters-in-law, grandchildren, and great-grandchildren. It was phenomenal! Out of selfishness for myself, I longed for her to pray for me, but I didn't want to inconvenience her. Although, deep down, I really wanted a final prayer from Mrs. Fraumann.

The day Mrs. Fraumann transitioned to heaven was sad. However, I/we knew she was at peace and welcomed her transition to heaven. When I left that evening, a little after 6:00 P.M., as I was driving home, I noticed a patch of clouds east of where I was driving. As I looked at the clouds, I thought of Mrs. Fraumann and that perhaps that day/evening would be the last time I would see her. I hoped it wouldn't be, but it was the last time.

As the clouds closed in, there appeared two rainbows. Two, I was amazed and thought to myself, Mrs. Fraumann had transitioned, and sadly she had transitioned.

Twenty minutes later I arrived home and Mr. Fraumann called me and told me that his "Sweetie" transitioned. I was quiet over the phone – choked up – and I prayed for Mrs. Fraumann/Mr. Fraumann when I hung up the phone.

Till this day, I still have Mrs. Fraumann's picture next to my grandmother, Clara Cooper's picture, on the mirror of my dresser. These two women are my role models of being spirit filled women with a true definition of a grandmother. When I wake up in the morning or go to sleep at night, I always glance over to the pictures of my grandmother and Janice. It brings a smile to my face. Both of these ladies are "<u>God's Angels</u>" here on earth. I love and miss you both.

Kathy Carothers
Caregiver

Jan Fraumann . . . from the moment I met her I knew someone special had come into my life! She presented to my clinic for counseling and care, yet I was the one transformed by her inner strength and grace. She had unwavering faith in dealing with life's adversities. She changed my world view and I'm a better person for having known her.

Claire Rice
Nurse

I first met Jan Fraumann on October 10, 2012. It started me on a long joyful, spiritual journey. Jan was an exceptional human being. I knew of Jan's medical history at the start of the case. I was already impressed by her courage and faith.

Over time, I came to learn about her extraordinary journey, in her own words. She truly knew her purpose in this world. She knew this purpose from an early age. This truly impressed me. She helped me understand that God remains with us always. When my husband developed heart problems, she helped me realize that Randy's life was in God's hands. We had many talks together. She encouraged and instructed me, in a new world of faith. I will always be appreciative of her support.

Jan Fraumann's legacy will be one of humility, grace, love, and kindness. I will continue to use her knowledge and wisdom in the coming years.

Eileen Poole
Caregiver

God's Blessed Angel

Jan Fraumann traveled a course very few people have ever navigated. I met her at Atlanta Orthopedic Specialists in Marietta, Georgia under the worst case scenario...she entered with unspecified leg pain and shortly after learned that she had an extremely rare and aggressive cancer. Throughout every twist, turn, and challenge, Jan radiated the strength and peace that is only possible through the assurance that no earthly matter would ever define her.

It was very apparent to me that Jan was going to live every day rejoicing for the blessings she treasured...her family, her many friends, and her faith in Christ. As a healthcare professional, I'm supposed to care and comfort, but in Jan's presence I often felt I was receiving more comfort than I offered. You see, Jan was filled with the fruit of the Spirit...love, joy, peace, patience, kindness, goodness and faithfulness.

God works in mysterious ways, and only He knows how many souls have been touched by Jan's amazing journey. I'm thankful my path crossed hers and we will meet again.

Gail Haley Smith
Nurse

Janice Fraumann

I had the wonderful opportunity to be Jan's occupational therapist on several occasions. It turned out we lived near the same street and we were able to stay in contact throughout the years. Jan was always an inspiration to those around her, working hard to stay independent, despite each new challenge sent her way. She was an active listener, always opening her heart and mind to others around her, regardless of her own pain.

Curious about my Jewish faith, we would talk about the similarities within our beliefs. She was in awe of the ritualistic prayers and blessings Jews have to pray over our children, and told me about adopting that into her everyday life, and sharing it with others.

It just felt good to be around Jan, and I will always be thankful that I had the opportunity to get to know this wonderful and unique woman.

Beth Janes
Occupational Therapist

God's Blessed Angel

It is not often that a person comes into your life at just the right time, as if their presence was part of God's plan. This is exactly what happened when I met Jan Fraumann. She had been in my office many times before, but for the first time several years ago, I became her doctor, responsible for caring for her eyes and vision, and she became my friend; my "Angel Sent By God".

When we first connected, I had just found out that my best friend and the love of my life, my mother, had been diagnosed with pancreatic cancer. Jan came in a day or two after I had learned of the devastating news, and I could hardly speak. As I teared up, Jan comforted me and gave me hope and inspiration that my mom and I would get through this. As she shared her experiences with me, she told me to tell my mother to never give up. I passed along her story of courageousness and faith in God to my mother.

Every time that Jan would visit the office, no matter what was going on with her own health, she always kept smiling and never let cancer defeat her soul. This made me feel at ease and enabled me to get through the hard times. Not being by my mother's side through all of this, because of the distance that separated us, left me feeling helpless, but Jan gave me strength to fill that void. Never once did she have a negative attitude, and even after her cancer returned, happiness and peacefulness seemed to surround her.

After two years of battling cancer, my mother passed away. On the day of the funeral, my two daughters and I stood on the front porch of my childhood home in Ohio, looked up at the sky and witnessed a triple rainbow so bright and vivid that I knew that my mother was sending us a message that she was okay and in a better place. Mr. Fraumann had stated that a double rainbow had appeared when Jan had passed, interestingly!

Looking back, I didn't realize how important Jan's presence had been in my life; an "Angel Sent By God" with a mission. Every time she would leave my office, I would hug her and always told her that I would pray for her. Being around her made me feel closer to my mother and to God.

Melissa Giannamore
Optometrist

Janice Fraumann

Jan was an amazing woman of God!

I had worked beside her in some difficult and challenging times and also some of the darkest times after her radical surgery.

What Jan consistently showed me and those around her was her love for Jesus, and her love for those God placed in her life. She was always patient and kind even though she was experiencing tremendous pain herself.

As a healthcare worker, I would often leave her room feeling like she helped me, more than I had helped her!

During her darkest times she requested no visitors, which did not seem like her, and that is when I began to pray more earnestly for her, knowing that evil was taunting her. I remember humming as I entered her room, "in this very room . . . Jesus, is in this very room" and "Jesus loves me." The simple tunes calmed her anxious fear and pain like nothing else.

I then began to share with Jan my journey of "A Thousand Gifts" by Amy Voskamp. I journaled three things I was thankful for and in a year I hoped to thank God for "one thousand gifts" He had given me. At my suggestion, Jan began journaling her thankful gifts, three every day, despite the pain and struggles she was experiencing.

Sometime later, I recall going to the dining hall to find her, and I was amazed at what I saw. Jan was surrounded by other residents and she was grinning from ear to ear saying, "It's Jesus who has given me the strength to stand on my polio leg. He is the one who has given me the courage and strength and energy to succeed."

That is when I saw living proof of God's promise in Isaiah 61:3, "To all who mourn in Israel, he will give a crown of beauty for ashes, a joyous blessing instead of mourning, festive praise instead of despair. In their righteousness, they will be like great oaks that the Lord has planted for His own glory."

Jan was like a mighty oak, always pointing upward to the power and glory of God. Her life was an inspiration to all who knew her. May it also be to those who hear and read her story!

Dolly Nielsen
Physical Therapist

God will use what He would not choose. Jan Fraumann brought that lesson home for those of us who were privileged to know her. Only the most mean-spirited of people could accuse God of causing Jan's cancer. God loved her too much, and she loved God too much for that to be a possibility. Jan understood that we live in a fallen world. As Christians, this earth is not our destination. Heaven and eternity with God is our future. While we are here, good and bad things happen to good and bad people, usually at the intersections of our freedom. Somewhere along the way whatever causes cancer ran into Jan and found a foothold and a ten year battle of body, mind, and spirit began.

The Bible talks a lot about suffering. One of the special kinds of suffering is "redemptive suffering." That is the kind of suffering which has been so completely surrendered to God that God can do one of His amazing reversals and make what is awful and terrible, wonder-full and awe-filled. Jan's suffering was like that. In the hospital, in rehab, in every setting, Jan made her love and confidence in God a natural part of her contacts with people who were trying to help her, and her suffering became a source of inspiration and courage.

I well remember the day she had her leg amputated. As she came out from under anesthesia, she smiled her big smile and said, "For the first time in nearly ten years, my body is cancer free! Thank God!"

Speaking in a phrase borrowed from one of my favorite preachers, there are those who might wish to say that cancer happened to Jan. As Jan's pastor, my opinion is that, by the grace of God, Jan happened to cancer, and cancer came off as the loser. We who observed the battle now know that the ultimate victor was not cancer. If a similar battle comes our way, we have had the privilege of seeing how a believer can deal with cancer.

No one should romanticize Jan's battle. She hurt like anybody else would. She experienced depression and doubt. She knew the agony of leaving her family prematurely and long nights of hard questions. But, as the hymn writer says, "Through it all ... she learned to trust in Jesus and learned to trust in God."

I am grateful that, among my private cloud of witnesses, Jan Fraumann will be a constant inspiration for the rest of my life.

Joe Peabody, Senior Pastor
Mt. Zion United Methodist Church 2009-2013

Jan's life deeply impacted so many people in our congregation. I met Jan in the midst of her battle with cancer, which was a time she was less present in the church. However, her name and her presence continued to be a powerful influence of spiritual leadership. Jan was a traditional southern Christian lady. She had married young to a man she admired and joined him in a lifetime of music ministry. She raised her sons and managed her home with all the charm and grace of a traditional happy homemaker.

Being raised in a different era of women's roles, I was not sure what Jan might think of me – an ordained woman, who worked full-time outside the home, while also being married to a man in ministry while trying to raise my children and manage my home. We were different women. From different eras. And yet, none of that mattered. We were women who loved and desired nothing more than allow the grace and joy of Christ to shine through our lives.

I always felt she deeply respected me and my calling, though I was living life so differently than she had. And I pray that she knew how deeply I respected her. A woman who lived exactly as she heard God call her to live. She taught me to look deeply into the hearts of others before making assumptions and judgments.

She taught me that women who feel called by God can lead very different lives, yet burn with the very same passion for Christ.

Laurie Moeller
Pastor

Should an artist sit to paint a vista of the life of Jan Fraumann selecting the natural beauty of God's creation, his selection of scenes would be his challenge.

He would choose the quiet morning sunrise of an oceanside where the sounds of waves and the blending colors cause the heart and mind to rejoice in beauty.

He would take his paint and board to a meadowed countryside of Ireland to capture the evenness of life unfolded in a distance full and strong, giving constant its joy.

Our artist would climb the roughed, dangerous and difficult mountainside somewhere in the Rockies, there to be paused for a while, to see that portion of life lost of vitality, hardly able to smile through the sunset.

Then he would search for that special scene where for sure the ocean waves and noise of time were more quiet, the landscapes more serene, and the rugged hills made plain. He would choose the hillside in a holy place where the Savior once laid lifeless for awhile then rose into life unending.

Finally, our artist would step back to see his work and rejoice, for he had been with Jan all through the journey and knew her well.

Hugh Cauthen
Pastor

It was my privilege to know Jan's parents and grandparents. We grew up as young teenagers in the same church, Sunday School and youth group in Columbus, GA, in the early 1950's.

There was in Jan a spiritual maturity which was greater than her chronological years. The way she dealt with her polio may have been a part of that depth of spirit. She had in her walk with Christ a genuineness, an authentic and personal relationship with the Lord.

Those who knew her recognized that she had an outgoing personality. She was a friend to everyone. Jan demonstrated to all of us that she had a "pure heart" like is mentioned in the Beatitudes, Matthew 5:8.

Jan knew who she was, therefore there was no trace of pretense. All the young people realized that she was very intelligent and yet, there a quality of innocence in her.

After we graduated high school, we went to Asbury (College) University, and made the long trip from Columbus, GA to Wilmore, KY, many times. When you grow up together, spend as much time together in church, and traveling back and forth to college, you get to know them very well. That is why I can say with all sincerity that Jan was a genuine Christian lady, who loved the Lord with all her heart!

Jim Rush
Minister

When I reflect upon the life of Jan Fraumann, three words come to mind; Faith, Family, and Friends. Obviously, it is difficult, nearly impossible to condense all of the memorable experiences of such a cherished and wonderful individual into a few paragraphs. However, these expressions are intended to paint a picture of a life more deserving than pen to paper could provide.

The Bible says, "**Faith** is the substance of things hoped for, the evidence of things not seen." Jan kept her eyes on the goal, even when circumstances would suggest that she do otherwise. Her faith was grounded not only in accepting Jesus as her Savior, but in the daily walk of trusting Him to work miracles. To say the least, she experienced a few of them during her lifetime. Without reservation, Jan "talked the talk" and "walked the walk." She was always hopeful, always praying, always trusting, always believing that God would see her through. This well lived life of unrelenting faith was an enormous blessing to me.

Family was a high priority for Jan. When I think of her, my thoughts move to Bob within the same second of time. Jan had a way of letting you know that they were inextricably connected. Her husband was the most important person in her life. Having children, grandchildren, and great-grandchildren were the enhanced dimension of life for her. While she dearly loved her own family, she was also concerned about the families of others. And, she wanted to know their children's names, ages, birthdays, grade levels, hobbies, when they met Christ, whether they were dating, when they were married, etc. The kind of interest in the life of a family other than her own, has left an indelible mark on my memory.

Friends were almost synonymous with family in Jan's eyes. Her kind, gentle, warm, tender, sensitive spirit was magnetic. Becoming Jan's friend meant being with her for life. She did not hesitate to bless you with her "southern charm". I will cherish the memory of one, who was the epitome of love, dedication, and faithfulness, Jan Fraumann.

Ralph Freeman
Friend

God's Blessed Angel

Our small group Bible study began ten years ago in the Fraumann home for a church-wide study of "40 Days of Purpose" by Rick Warren. We all knew Bob as our Music Minister, but most of us did not know Jan. It did not take long for us to realize that God had put us together under Jan's leading for a very good reason! Jan took us under her wing, and through her unique and powerful testimony, encouraged us as we began a closer walk with our Lord. We always left on Monday night feeling inspired to live our faith the way Jan demonstrated every day.

She challenged us to write out our testimony, to be bold, to study the Word, to pray often and fervently (and out loud!) and to ask God for favor and protection on ourselves and our family. Through surgeries and treatment, Jan continued to be a "good and faithful servant" and poured herself into every book we studied, adding her own perspective in her own humble manner. She would talk and we would listen! In doing so, we stretched our own comfort zones and our individual faith journeys grew as a result.

Jan also taught us to praise God even in the storms of life. Through her illness she leaned on God and not her own understanding. She often said that she was not special, but she was wrong about that. She was a treasure to us and to so many. We felt especially blessed because we spent time with her every Monday night! She made each of us feel special, and encouraged us through our life's challenges, even when her own were weighing on her. On occasion she prayed for us on the phone, she anointed us with oil and blessed us and taught us the power of laying hands on someone who needed special prayer. When we visited Jan in the hospital after her amputation, she ministered to us more so than we did to her!

Jan's passion for the Lord, her laughter, her love for family and church family will live on in our hearts forever. She inspired us beyond measure. She was our mentor, our friend, our hero. Our Monday night family carries on in her memory. What a true privilege it was for each of us to know her, to love her and to be loved by her. Always in our hearts – our dear Jan.

Monday Night Bible Study Friends - Kathy Gyselinck, Janet and Jeff Hamm, Penny and David King, Kathy and Dave Moore

160

My reflections on Jan take me to the first time I met her. My husband and I decided to join a Bible study group at Mt. Zion United Methodist Church. This was our first experience participating in a Bible study group so we weren't sure what to expect. Upon entering the room, Jan and Bob Fraumann were the first couple to greet us. All anxiety melted away with Jan's warm smile and Bob's welcoming manner. At that point, Jan was five years into her challenging health journey, but there was no indication that she was in the fight of her life. She was always "put together" from head to toe with a calm, kind demeanor that only comes from knowing that God has a plan and He is in charge.

Her knowledge of the Bible was impressive, as she clearly used it as her guide in living her life. Jan was full of wisdom that she was happy to share, and we often looked to Jan for interpretation, when we struggled with certain passages in the Bible. <u>To be close to Jan was to be close to God</u>.

Jan had a grace about her that was an inspiration to all who knew her, and definitely lived by example. I feel very blessed to have Jan as my dear friend and I miss being in her presence and the joy she shared. I'm a better person for having known Jan, as she has instilled in me the desire to use the Bible as my guide and continue to grow in my personal relationship with God. I miss you, dear friend, but know that you are in a wonderful place.

Suzanne Decker
Friend

In this world and in this life and in this generation, for me it is rare to find, let alone have a chance to even know a person like Jan Fraumann. Mine was sheer luck, or was it, when Suzanne and I joined a small, newly forming Bible study class at Mt. Zion United Methodist Church. Jan and Bob were there. Over the many months, whenever a subject came up about faith, or doing the right thing, or what God expects of us, or what the Bible says about something, I was always thankful when Jan was there.

She had such a knowledgeable, loving, true, and comforting way about her. I always was interested in Jan's thoughts on things and how she so easily and confidently spoke about life, the Bible, her faith, Jesus, and God. Without her even knowing it, she taught me so much. Along with so many other things, I learned how a brave, and dignified woman deals with adversity and death. More importantly, she showed me what a true Christian looks like and what real faith feels like. I love Jan Fraumann.

Brett Decker
Friend

Jan showed her love of God in everything she did. I was blessed to know her first as a spiritual teacher, then as a dear friend, full of compassion, understanding, wisdom, and love. I am so grateful for the times we spent together and on the phone. She was my closest friend, the one I could confide in and the first one I would want to share news with.

Through the blessing class, she encouraged me to pray out loud for my granddaughters and family. She prayed once that I would "thirst" for the Word of God. And, I believe that led me to a more faithful devotion time.

I felt privileged to help her during her illness and especially to see her and pray for her a few days before her passing. She was beautiful, inside and out, a very special friend, more like a sister to me, and the perfect example of how a Christian should live their life. I thank God for Jan and our special friendship. "She Was A Blessing, An Angel On Earth". I think of her and miss her every day.

Sharon Humphrey
Friend

I've loved Jan since I first met her back in 1984, when Bob came to Mt. Zion United Methodist Church, Marietta, Georgia, as Director of Music. She has been an inspiration to Rick and me ever since, and "A Gift From God". When the contemporary service was first started at Mt. Zion about fourteen years ago, I was allowed to join the praise team. The service was at 9:45, so the Team wasn't available for Sunday School. As a result, Jan took it upon herself to suggest we all meet on Friday evenings at their home as a small group, which included her and Bob. We know that the Lord led Jan to suggest that, and we were truly blessed and fed as a result.

The Lord used Jan to teach us many things, and prayer was right at the top of the list. She was a precious friend, a true prayer warrior, and "God's Gift To Us".

Donna and Rick Rice
Friends

I first met Jan over ten years ago when she taught the blessings class, and from there spent Sunday nights in small group with her and Bob. I knew from the first time I met her that she was a very special person.

Her love of the Lord was unwavering and powerful, I had never met anyone like her before. She had a gift for making you feel special and always offered words of encouragement, even when she wasn't feeling well. Her insight and wisdom of the Bible made her a wonderful teacher and leader.

I feel so blessed to have known Jan. She was the single most important person in my life in terms of my spiritual growth and development. I miss her terribly, but know she is with the Lord, smiling down on Bob and her family.

Judy Bush
Friend

Most precious Jan, we sure miss you here. You always had so many uplifting things to say to brighten anyone's day, even when you did not feel well. You never complained about feeling bad and your face did not give up your secret.

<u>In Bible studies, anytime you would speak, the entire class would become so quiet (you could hear a pin drop) because we knew what you were saying was the truth given by God</u>. And, there were several evenings after Bible study when you would invite an individual or couple to remain to further discuss a specific issue they were dealing with. This was in spite of fatigue and/or pain.

Your gift of prayer was spirit-filled and we always appreciated when you prayed, whether for an individual or a group. I miss your beautiful smile and spiritual guidance, but most of all I miss you. I know you are in a wonderful place with your Lord who has made you whole and reunited with your family. God is truly blessed to have you there. I love you Jan.

Your sister in Christ,

Kathy Gyselinck
Friend

Janice Fraumann

We learned so much from Jan. She walked and talked by faith, and was led by her personal relationship with the Lord. She shared her testimony with joy.

Jan knew the importance of "God's Blessings" and was called to teach others how to do it also. Jan was a real prayer warrior and we often went to her with our personal prayer needs. As we strive to grow in faith and to influence future generations, Jan is still an important guide and example.

David and Penny King
Friends

Jan Fraumann came into my life as an "Unexpected Blessing From God". It is impossible to talk about Jan without including the love of her life, Bob. I always loved seeing them together. I loved watching her beautiful smile and listening to her laugh at Bob's jokes. They had fun together and made it fun for everyone to be around them. Their marriage was an inspiring example.

I had the pleasure and honor of being their insurance agent. Right from the beginning they made me feel special and that I was important to them. I soon realized that they had the gift of making everyone feel special. The love and joy of God showed in everything they did.

Through all of Jan's illnesses, she showed great dignity and grace. She always gave thanks to God and never dwelled on herself. She believed in giving thanks in all circumstances. Jan taught classes on blessing others, but she was the blessing to all of us who knew her. She is so missed, but we will see her again. Jan makes the thought of Heaven even sweeter.

Sheila Geist
Insurance Agent

Janice Fraumann

I have been struggling to find words to express my thoughts and memories of you, my dear Jan, to put down on paper. So many memories! I just want you to know how much you meant to me, in the conversations we had. I remember seeing you speak many years ago at a business meeting. Jack and I met you and your love, Bob, in the seventies, and we became special friends. You always made me feel so good with your positive input. You knew me so well, and I appreciated that more than you know. You were a beautiful person inside and out. I remember my last visit with you. You wanted me to join The Well (ladies group at church), which I did. I will always cherish and love you in my memories. Until we meet again.

Love,
Betty Derham
Business Associate

I will always remember Jan as the greatest prayer warrior I have ever known. It did not matter how ill she was or her condition, she was always there in prayer for others.

Jan was a beautiful lady, both inside and out. She is my hero. I will always be thankful to God for her. I look forward to our next meeting together in heaven.

Sisters In Christ,
Karen Kuntz
Friend

Jan was a wonderful role model of a godly woman. Kindness and wisdom came from her just when I needed it most. I'll always remember her practical method for gently, but firmly discouraging others from gossiping to her.

Jan possessed great singing ability about which she never boasted, but gave God the glory. She was gracious and loving. I count it a great privilege to have known Jan Fraumann.

Karen Strothers
Friend

I knew Jan for several years, but you only had to talk with her for a few minutes, to see she was a real Christian. I cherish the times we talked about the Bible, and prayed for her healing. Although she was in pain, she never complained. She was the most godly person I ever knew. I miss her and look forward to seeing her in heaven.

Kathy and Farrow Walls
Friends

There is and always will be a special place in my heart that only my dear and wonderful friend Jan can fill.

If I were to do a patch quilt of friends, Jan's patch would be:

- ❖ White background for her purity of mind, soul, and spirit.
- ❖ Pink and purple array of beautiful spring flowers in the center.
- ❖ Pink for her beauty and grace.
- ❖ Purple for her regal manner that radiated when you were in her presence.
- ❖ Gold border to represent the golden rays of sunshine that brought joy and warmth to all she knew.

I will miss Jan very much. However, the many happy memories (four of us backstage hosting business functions with Bob and Jan, having the best fried fish in the Florida docks at New Smyrna Beach, and our beautiful Kentucky weekend with friends, Bill and Diane Williams,) we shared will never be forgotten and I will cherish them forever.

Love you Jan!

Daveine Wendt
Business Associate

What an honor to be a part of this wonderful act of love by Bob Fraumann as he completes Jan's biography. I admired the talented Fraumann family before we became close friends. Then, we grew to appreciate their hearts and love for the Lord.

As Jan began her treatments for cancer, she spoke often about writing a book about what God has done in her life, and now Bob has done it.

Her life is an example, to a younger generation who are being taught to seek success and happiness in many other ways, that God will bless and use a life committed to Him.

Thank you, Jan and Bob, for what I know is a wonderfully inspiring story.

Diane and Bill Williams
Business Associates

I don't remember exactly when I first began getting to know Jan because I feel like I've known her all my life. She welcomed me into her life without reservation. Jan had a way of always making you feel like you were special to her because you were. Everyone was special to Jan.

Jan cared for people and especially for their spiritual life and their relationship with Christ. I loved being in Bible study with her. Her insight always helped me see things in a different way. She always encouraged me when I led a Bible study.

She asked me once if I had a message for her from God. I know I must have had a blank look on my face, but she didn't take her eyes off me as she asked me again if I had a word for her from God. I told her that I didn't know of anything that God had asked me to tell her, but it really made me more aware of listening to God, because He just might ask me to give someone a message.

Jan was a friend, a mentor, and an encourager. I was blessed to know her and call her my friend.

Tani Gilliam
Friend

It is impossible to put into words how blessed we have been by knowing Bob and Jan Fraumann for over forty years. Jan has had such a positive influence in our lives. The very first time we saw her, we thought she was so beautiful and glamorous, with a faithful spirit that was contagious. She was always happy, always positive, and always wanting those around her to be the same. Jan was the epitome of grace, dignity, faith and mercy.

There were many times in our lives when she seemed to have just the right words or the right advice. She wanted all around her to never be jealous, never envious, and to be forgiving and thankful for everything, good or bad. Jan always thought of others first, even near death, insisting she pray for her family, rather than prayer for her.

Deb: I remember when we were in our twenties (the seventies seemed like a long time ago) and we were attending an important business meeting with Bob and Jan. I suffered from migraines and was hiding out in the ladies room. Well, Jan found me and gave me a stern talking to and let me know in Jan's loving way that I should be sitting with my husband and giving him support instead of hiding out. Of course, I listened and will never forget that important lesson from the heart. I always looked up to Jan with the utmost respect and was always eager to listen to her womanly advice. She was a beautiful lady, inside and out, and I always strive to be just like her. Her laughter I will never forget. I have so many wonderful memories that I will cherish in my heart. Love you, Jan.

We miss Jan, but we are comforted in knowing that we will see her beautiful smile again. Her love and compassion lives on through Bob, who has love and encouragement for all around him. God truly has blessed us with their true friendship through all these years.

Don and Debbie Evans
Business Associates

Jan has reached her reward: her years of pain has passed. She loved her Lord, her family, and her friends – totally – in that order.

How blessed and grateful we are for the memories of many traveled miles and special times we have spent with her.

Lindell and Ann DeJarnett
Business Associates

God's Blessed Angel

To tell anyone how wonderful Jan Fraumann was would take a book, at least. And, that is the enormous task my friend, Bob, has taken. Accordingly, I will share a couple of small stories about her that will give but a glimpse of what she meant to me and my family. Because it involves my daughter, I have chosen to remain anonymous.

In the year before her passing, Jan had lost a leg in a battle against cancer. I recall visiting her and instantly tearing up at the sight and thought of her suffering. Astonishingly, she began to laugh and said: "This is what I have been praying for. I asked God to remove the cancer, and it's gone." In the midst of her struggles, there she was, as always, seeking to comfort those around her. She reached out for my hand and asked about my college-aged daughter. Earlier, I had confided to her that my only child was not walking with God, and had succumbed to the temptations of college life. I told Jan I prayed every day for my only child. Jan told me she did, too. She began a prayer that was more of a request for a blessing than a petition to the Lord. My daughter called that evening. I told her I loved her and I had been praying for her. She said, that she had been praying lately, too.

A few weeks later, Jan spoke at the United Methodist Women's Sunday Service at our church (chapter three) and invited those in the congregation to come up after the service and pray with her about any of our concerns. After several others had prayed with Jan, (she was worth the wait), she smiled at me as if she knew exactly what was on my mind. Before I could say anything, my wife interjected that I was going to see a doctor the next morning about a small lump I had found in my body. Jan grabbed both our hands and prayed for my health, and without prompting, also prayed for our daughter. She knew exactly what we needed. At my visit with my doctor the next morning, after a thorough examination (too thorough if you ask me), there was nothing. The lump had disappeared. The doctor explained in clinical terms how this was possible. But, I had another explanation.

I talk and text with my daughter often. And, yes, she is walking with God.

Jan was an inspiration to all who knew her. She had a knowledge and understanding of people and business and knew how to combine them for success. She was a guide and mentor to Anita and me the many years we knew her. We enjoyed many good times together with Jan and family at the beach. Wherever we were, in the pool, dining out, or just sitting around talking, was more exciting with Jan there. Shopping in New York, or the islands when on a cruise, or any weekend retreat, had to include much time looking at all the jewelry and trying on expensive, outlandish outfits. She made sure everyone had fun!

She had great musical talent which was devoted to God and shared freely with others. Our lives have been enriched through our association with Jan and her family. She will be missed by all who knew her and will always be remembered with love and affection.

Mac (Horace) and Anita McFarland
Business Associates

God's Blessed Angel

Jan, Bob and adorable three year old Ricky came to First United Methodist Church in East Point, Georgia when Bob joined the staff as Minister of Music in 1963. We were most fortunate in finding them in Kentucky, wanting to move south. All of us were most favorably impressed with them and became friends instantly!

Jan had a marvelous solo contralto voice and added greatly to the choir. Also, her speaking voice was quite melodious. Jan was always cheerful and positive---a real joy to all. My daughter remembers her beauty and that her hair, makeup, and wardrobe were very stylish!

Jan was a gentle person, a true "southern lady"! We are blessed to have known and loved her!

Peggy Hardin
Friend

Janice Fraumann

Jan Frauman. What a beautiful LADY! It is hard to put into words how special Jan was. She was someone others could look up to with respect and admiration. She always had a smile, a kind word, a gentle hand...a hug. There was nothing false about her. She never said anything bad about anyone, in fact, she always looked for the good. Above all, she was the true meaning of a Christian.

Any time you were around her, you felt a peace...a peace only God could give to you. Jan brought so many to Christ through her actions, words and music. She spent so much time with the Lord in prayer and learning His Word. Now Jan is with the Lord. What a blessing it was to know her.

Lynn Hummer
Friend

Jan was a good-hearted soul who blessed everyone's life she touched. She was a great wife, wonderful mother, sharp talented business woman, active leader in her church and community, a talented musician and most of all a precious loving friend who NEVER spoke an unkind word about anyone and always thought of others first.

One profound example of Jan's spirit happened when she lost her leg to cancer. Bob walked into her hospital room fearful of how he would console Jan over the loss of her leg. Jan turned and looked at Bob with a sweet smile on her face and said "Now, Bob, I will be able to ride in the front seat with you again!"

Another time I overheard Jan speaking to a customer of the credit business she owned. This man was late on his payments and was not very kind to Jan. So what did she do? Jan gently thanked him for being a customer, and spoke with profound kindness that she was sure he would honor his commitment and make his payment, as agreed, and that she understood his challenge and *how could she help him*! Before the conversation was over, this irate person's entire attitude had changed to gratitude. Jan had a way about her that caused people to be their best!

Jan is missed by everyone who knew her! Jan was an example of how to live when you love the Lord with all your heart. She inspired me in so many ways!

Jan's friends will love and cherish this book, strangers who read this book will be blessed by the life and memories of Janice Brown Fraumann. So share this book!

Bobbie Stam Boyken
Business Associate

Janice Fraumann

My wife and I knew Jan Fraumann for more than three decades and had the privilege of working and traveling alongside her as she built two thriving businesses, developed a strong family and served her church and community. What an inspiration to see her overcome a horrible medical condition in childhood and another in later life without complaint, but with confident Christian joy. Truly her children—and many others – "<u>Rise And Call Her Blessed</u>."

Dr. Dorsey M. and Pam Deaton
Business Associates

Rory and I met Jan through her son Greg, who moved to the Canton, Ohio area when he met and got engaged to his future wife, Terri. The things that impressed us both about this true "southern lady" were her love for the Lord and her love for her family. It wasn't easy for Jan to have her boys living away, but the most important thing for her was that they be where the Lord wanted them to be. It warmed her heart to know that Terri loved Greg dearly, and to see that love grow as the years passed, and their family grew with the addition of two beautiful girls.

One of the last times we had with Jan was at the home of Greg and Terri. We were in the piano room singing Christmas carols and Jan was asked to sing. I had never heard Jan sing. What a beautiful blessing God had in store for me that evening as I saw the look on her face, the sparkle in her eyes, especially when she looked at her son. My heart was overwhelmed with blessings that evening that I will treasure always.

Jan's courage as she battled illness, continuing to take life one day at a time, and loving her Savior through it, was and is an inspiration to me and I am sure everyone who had the privilege to come in contact with her. There were dark and difficult days, but Jesus had the victory.

1 Corinthians 15:57 - But thanks be to God, which giveth us the victory through our Lord Jesus Christ.

Rory and Pat Wineka
Friends

Jan Fraumann: A beautiful, unforgettable lady. We met Jan and Bob in 1972 when they came to our home in Tiny Town, TN and we became and still are business associates.

Jan had an angelic voice, and a smile that always lit up the room. I learned so much from Jan. She taught me to always speak well of everyone. She truly loved her friends and family like Jesus said, "Love your neighbor as yourself." I was always impressed by the way her clothing, jewelry makeup and everything coordinated. She always reminded me of a fashion model. I asked her one time how she managed to have so many lovely clothes, etc. and she said, "I watch for sales." To me, Jan was the perfect example of a wife, mother, and business partner.

Our lives have been truly blessed by knowing Jan.

Vera and Kirk Kirkpatrick
Business Associates

It is said that behind every successful man there is a strong and supportive woman. Jan Fraumann was and her spirit is the strength behind the talents and ministry of her loving husband, Bob. Jan and I both liked sitting toward the back of the sanctuary, and every Sunday I watched Jan be the first to her feet to applaud Bob's music and the first to her knees in prayer. Bob and Jan's marriage was truly made in heaven.

Senator Johnny Isakson

Janice Fraumann

Jan Fraumann was an inspiration to so many people! She was a wonderful teacher and spiritual leader in our Monday night Bible study. Dan remembers how Jan helped him with sharing his faith experiences, so that God alone would be glorified.

Jan's courage during her battle with cancer inspired all who knew her. We visited Jan at Crawford Long hospital a couple of days after she lost her leg, and we left her hospital room as the ones who were encouraged! Her ability to communicate the use of the power of the Holy Spirit in our lives was truly remarkable!

Becca recalled how much it meant to her the day that Jan called and prayed with her after Becca's father passed away.

Jan was such a positive and encouraging Christian role model as a loving wife, mother, grandmother and great-grandmother. She was such a loyal friend. Jan's legacy and Christian influence will surely be evident in future generations. She was truly a saint of saints.

Dan and Becca Farr
Friends

The Gift of a Holy Woman. For many years I wrote stories, based on "special gifts", as a Christmas gift for family and friends. Recently, thoughts of a special gift kept flowing through my mind, like a new melody that wouldn't let go! It occurred to me . . . sometimes like music... thoughts and memories need to be expressed, Christmas or not!

I first saw her in the choir at Sandy Springs United Methodist Church, Atlanta, Georgia, in 1980. Yes, Jan Fraumann was beautiful . . . yes, her voice was beautiful, and yes, her spirit was warm and inviting . . . but there was no doubt in my mind, and I knew in an instant . . . she was real! As the many years passed, and our lives touched through friendship and music, I came to understand that God had shared, from the "Realms of Glory," one of His angels for the benefit of those who knew her here on earth. Oh, the many people she touched, starting with her home family and her church family; not to speak of strangers (who soon were not!) There was nothing about her that didn't point to THE WAY, THE TRUTH and THE LIGHT, even while she had to carry heavier burdens than most can imagine . . . burdens that did not pass away here on this earth.

All of us were the "Blessed Ones" . . . she showed us the way! She was a holy woman . . . a special "*Gift From God*"! Selah!

Beverly Smith Herrington
Friend

Chapter Fifteen
Blessing Thoughts from Jan

Jewish Traditions

We have Biblical history of blessings with Jewish families. Why do we not have Christian families using blessings? Rewards go with the blessing.

Jan said: "It has been my goal to be a good wife and mother. I have attended many seminars, and read many books on the subject. Why had I missed the blessing? It was a big piece of the puzzle. We were constantly looking for ways to have a better home life. The blessing escaped us. Why have we never heard about it?"

The blessing seems to be a major missing piece of the puzzle in our Christian lives and families.

Of course, the Bible teaches stories about Jesus and parents blessing children. But, have we ever done it?

Blessings must be spoken! You can say a blessing you've thought about. You can also write a blessing and speak it over your child. The reason you must contemplate what you say is because:

1. You do not want any negatives in your blessing.
2. Every sentence must be positive.
3. The blessing will have a great impact upon your child.
4. We believe God's power is in the blessing.

Janice Fraumann

"No negatives."
Be sure you word every blessing in a positive way.

NO: May God bless you and help you not to make bad grades.
YES: May God bless you and help you to make good grades.

NO: May God bless you and keep you from fighting with your
        brothers and sisters.
YES: May God bless you and give you a desire to get along well
        with your brothers and sisters.

NO: May God keep you from lack and poverty.
YES: May God bless you with abundance of all good things.

NO: May God bless you and keep you from being mean to your
        sister.
YES: May God bless you and may you be kind and loving to your
        sister. May you share with your sister.

NO: May we be safe from burglars.
YES: May God give us (our family) and home divine protection over
        our minds, bodies, homes, auto, and possessions.

NO: Why can't you obey like your sister?
YES: May God help you obey your parents, teachers, and elders
        because they want the best for you.

DON'T PRAY: "God bless what I want to do."
DO PRAY: "God help me to do what You are blessing."

Examples of Spoken Blessings in the Bible

God/Adam
Genesis 1:26-28 (KJV)

And God said, Let us make man in our image, after our likeness: and let them have dominion over the fish of the sea, and over the fowl of the air, and over the cattle, and over all the earth, and over every creeping thing that creepeth upon the earth. So God created man in his own image, in the image of God created he him; male and female created he them. And God blessed them, and God said unto them, Be fruitful, and multiply, and replenish the earth, and subdue it: and have dominion over the fish of the sea, and over the fowl of the air, and over every living thing that moveth upon the earth.

Blessing on Heaven and Earth
Genesis 2:2-3 (KJV)

And on the seventh day God ended his work which he had made; and he rested on the seventh day from all his work which he had made. And God blessed the seventh day, and sanctified it: because that in it he had rested from all his work which God created and made.

Blessing of Isaac over Jacob
Genesis 27:26-29 (KJV)

And his father Isaac said unto him, Come near now, and kiss me, my son. And he came near, and kissed him: and he smelled the smell of his raiment, and blessed him, and said, See, the smell of my son is as the smell of a field which the LORD hath blessed: Therefore God give thee of the dew of heaven, and the fatness of the earth, and plenty of corn and wine: Let people serve thee, and nations bow down to thee: be lord over thy brethren, and let thy mother's sons bow down to thee: cursed be every one that curseth thee, and blessed be he that blesseth thee.

The Beatitudes
Matthew 5:3-11 (KJV)

Blessed are the poor in spirit: for theirs is the kingdom of
heaven.
Blessed are they that mourn: for they shall be comforted.
Blessed are the meek: for they shall inherit the earth.
Blessed are they which do hunger and thirst after
righteousness: for they shall be filled.
Blessed are the merciful: for they shall obtain mercy.
Blessed are the pure in heart: for they shall see God.
Blessed are the peacemakers: for they shall be called the
children of God.
Blessed are they which are persecuted for righteousness' sake:
for theirs is the kingdom of heaven.
Blessed are ye, when men shall revile you, and persecute you,
and shall say all manner of evil against you falsely, for
my sake.

Blessing – Ascension
Luke 24:50-53 (KJV)

And he led them out as far as to Bethany, and he lifted up his
hands, and blessed them. And it came to pass, while he blessed
them, he was parted from them, and carried up into heaven.
And they worshipped him, and returned to Jerusalem with great
joy: And were continually in the temple, praising and blessing
God. Amen.

Chapter Sixteen
Blessing Thoughts from Bob (The Author)

Bob's mother prayed a blessing on him every day before he went to school. She prayed a blessing for getting along with teachers and friends, for his safety, to learn his subject material, and for having a good day.

When Jan taught her classes, most students had never had this experience, or did not have any idea of how to do it.

First of all, we do know from the Bible that <u>blessings</u> and <u>curses</u> are generational. That being the case, decide <u>now</u>, to end any <u>curses</u> that may be generational. Begin now a generational blessing that will be the beginning of your legacy.

You may be asking, how?

The head of the household, whomever that may be, places his/her hands on the head and shoulder of the child/person, and speaks a blessing in the name of the Lord. There is power in the blessing. As an example, all through the Old Testament, God spoke many blessings.

The first two blessings in the Bible and the blessing at the Ascension are:

- Genesis 1:26-28 – The blessing on Adam and Eve
- Genesis 2:2-3 – The blessing on heaven and earth
- Luke 24:50-53 – The blessing on the Ascension

The first act of Jesus was the Beatitudes, Matthew 5:3-11.

The Jews blessed all their activities, and still do today.

You can always use The Priestly Blessing (Numbers 6:22-26, (see Chapter Twenty.)) God did it – why not us – you – me?

At the end of this book are beautiful sample blessings (5x7).
They can be cut out and framed.
If you would like to have a full color 8½x11 blessing, order at:

www.bobfraumann.com/blessings.htm.

Chapter Seventeen
Three Blessings a Day

Dolly Nielson, Jan's physical therapist at Manor Care, in Marietta, GA, suggested that Jan write three blessings a day based on the following book, "One Thousand Gifts," by Ann Voskamp.

"I went to Sweet Spirit Christian Book Store in Marietta to find a journal for Jan to write her blessings. Her amputation was on January 13, 2012. This journal begins on February 29, 2012 during the lowest time in her life. Jan certainly lived above circumstances, and trusted the Lord, as you will witness in the following sample entries." *Bob*

- I am thankful for Bob. He is so wonderful, concerned and faithful. He has been with me each step of the way and continues to be there for me.
- I am thankful for Greg. He came to be with me for the surgery and stayed a week with me, and was a great encouragement to Bob.
- I am thankful for Rick. He came to be with me after surgery. He was an encouragement to Bob also.
- I am thankful for Dolly Nielson, my physical therapist. Her verse for me today is Second Corinthians 4:8-9.

196

- I am thankful for Beth Janes, my occupational therapist. She is such an encouragement to me.
- I am thankful I am able to stand on a walker.
- I am thankful for friends and family who fixed my pajamas with one leg.
- Thank you God for faith filled words I can use to stay strong. My polio leg is getting stronger.
- Day by day in every way I am better and better.
- Thank you God that I was able to stand at the bars for three minutes. My goal is five minutes.
- I thank God that Bob is strong. He is bringing B.A.S.I.C.S. (youth choir) to sing for me. Bob, you are so terrific.
- I am thankful for many friends that visit me.
- I am thankful for church friends.
- I am thankful my body is getting stronger.
- My Bible study is coming to visit me and do the Bible study here at Manor Care.
- I am thankful for those who are helping Bob get the house ready, especially Danny Hummer, when I go home.
- I am thankful to God I met a Russian lady doctor today and I was able to witness to her.
- Praise God I was able to hop at the bars today.
- I was in the wheelchair for six hours today. Praise the Lord!
- Thank you nurses for all you do for me.
- Thank you, Julie LaFond, my niece, for taking care of my mother, Mama Mae.
- I love music which lifts my spirits.
- I'm thankful for the antibiotics which are killing the infection.
- Thanks that my physical therapy is going well.
- Bob is my dearest treasure! I love him so much. He brought me a bunch of fruit and goodies today.
- I am thankful for all of the beautiful flowers.

This list goes on and on with over four hundred entries. I hope this is an inspiration to you, no matter what your situation. God is able to supply all your needs. Endeavor to find three things to be thankful for each day, and begin your journal today with three blessings daily! This will be your inspiration. Guaranteed!!!

Chapter Eighteen
Scriptures with Blessings

<u>Old Testament</u>

Genesis 1:27-28a (KJV)
So God created man in His own image, in the image of God created he him, male and female created he them. And God blessed them.

Genesis 2:3 (KJV)
And God blessed the seventh day and sanctified it.

Genesis 9:1 (KJV)
And God blessed Noah and his sons, and said unto them, be fruitful and multiply and replenish the earth.

Genesis 12:2 (KJV)
And I will make of thee a great nation, and I will bless thee, and make thy name great; and thou shalt be a blessing.

Numbers 6:24-26 – The Priestly Blessing
The Lord bless you and keep you; the Lord make His face to shine upon you and be gracious to you; the Lord turn His face toward you and give you peace.

First Chronicles 4:10 (KJV)
And Jabez called on the God of Israel, saying, oh that thou wouldest bless me indeed, and enlarge my coast, and that thine hand might be with me, and that thou wouldest keep me from evil, that it may not grieve me! And God granted him that which he requested.

Psalm 3:8 (KJV)
Salvation belongeth to the Lord. Thy blessing is upon thy people.

Psalm 33:12a (KJV)
Blessed is the nation whose God is the Lord.

Psalm 28:9a (KJV)
Save thy people, and bless thine inheritance.

Psalm 68:19 (KJV)
Blessed be the Lord, who daily loadeth us with benefits, even the God of our salvation.

Psalm 128:1a (KJV)
Blessed is every one that feareth the Lord.

Proverbs 10:22 (KJV)
The blessing of the Lord, it maketh rich, and He addeth no sorrow to it.

<u>New Testament</u>

Matthew 5:3-11 (KJV)
(THE BEATITUDES)
Blessed are the poor in spirit: for theirs is the kingdom of heaven.

Blessed are they that mourn: for they shall be comforted.

Blessed are the meek: for they shall inherit the earth.

Blessed are they which do hunger and thirst after righteousness: for they shall be filled.

Blessed are the merciful: for they shall obtain mercy.

Blessed are the pure in heart: for they shall see God.

Blessed are the peacemakers: for they shall be called the children of God.

Blessed are they which are persecuted for righteousness' sake: for theirs is the kingdom of heaven.

Blessed are ye, when men shall revile you, and persecute you, and shall say all manner of evil against you falsely, for my sake.

Luke 1:28 (KJV)
And the angel came in unto her, and said, Hail, thou art highly favored, the Lord is with thee: blessed art thou among women.

Luke 24:50 (KJV)
And He led them out as far as to Bethany, and He lifted up His hands and blessed them.

Chapter Nineteen
Sample One Liner Blessing Ideas
That Jan Noted

❖ May you keep God first in your life.

❖ May you always have a tender heart toward God.

❖ May you keep a childlike faith in God.

❖ May you develop the strength and discipline of a warrior for Christ.

❖ May you have favor in those of high estate and low estate all your life.

❖ May God shine His blessing on you and your children and your children's children.

❖ May God's presence go with you.

❖ May God give you extremely good health and long life.

❖ May you have great vigor and stamina and enthusiasm for the work of the Lord.

❖ May God give you courage and holy boldness.

❖ May God give you tact in dealing with others.

❖ May you be a peacemaker.

❖ May God bless those who bless you.

❖ May God give you wisdom, knowledge, and understanding.

❖ May you be called a great leader among men.

❖ May God give you the desires of your heart.

❖ May you seek and accomplish God's calling and purpose for your life

❖ May you be blessed and also be a blessing to others.

❖ May God's protection be upon your body, soul, mind, and spirit.

❖ May God give you great reasoning power and the ability to express yourself well.

❖ May God give you the ability to communicate well with others.

❖ May God bless you with love and faithfulness so that you will win favor and a good name in the sight of God and man. Proverbs 3:3-4

❖ May you acknowledge God in all your ways, so that He will direct your ways. Proverbs 3:6

❖ May God give you the spirit of discernment.

❖ May God strengthen you and protect you from the evil one. Second Thessalonians 3:3

❖ May God bless you with a strong desire to please Him.

❖ May God give you ability to stand for godly principles and let your light shine in a darkened world. Matthew 5:16

❖ May God give you a spirit of compassion for those less fortunate.

❖ May God give you a spirit of giving, not just getting.

❖ May God give you true Christian friends.

❖ May you always know that God can wash away your sins so that you can be whiter than snow. Psalm 51:7

❖ May you trust in God when you are afraid,. Psalm 56:3-4

❖ May God bless you and keep you free from any addiction – especially alcohol or drugs. May God enable you to give Him control of your life.

❖ May God give you discernment and strength to say "no" to things that bring death and "yes" to things that bring life and blessing to you.

❖ May God protect and surround you with His shield of protection. No weapon formed against you shall prosper. Isaiah 54:17

❖ May God keep you under His umbrella of protection and may you walk in obedience.

Chapter Twenty

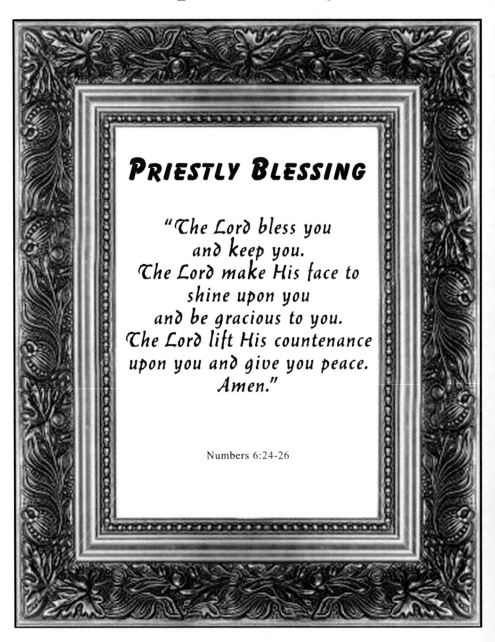

PRIESTLY BLESSING

"The Lord bless you
and keep you.
The Lord make His face to
shine upon you
and be gracious to you.
The Lord lift His countenance
upon you and give you peace.
Amen."

Numbers 6:24-26

Chapter Twenty-One

Sample Blessings

- Following are blessing samples for you to use. You can write more for any occasion.

- These 5x7 blessings can be cut out and framed.

- These are available in 8½x11 color.
  Order at www.bobfraumann.com/blessings.htm.

Enjoy.

May God bless you as you grow in your faith,
and become a blessing to everyone with whom you associate.

MARRIAGE BLESSING

MAY GOD BLESS OUR MARRIAGE, OUR
FAMILY AND OUR HOME.

MAY GOD EMPOWER US TO SEEK HIM FIRST.

MAY GOD GUIDE, DIRECT AND KEEP US
IN ALL OUR WAYS.

MAY GOD GRANT US WISDOM, HEALTH AND
PROSPERITY, EVEN AS OUR SOULS PROSPER.

MAY GOD BLESS US WITH LONG LIFE TOGETHER
AND ALLOW US TO LIVE
TOGETHER ETERNALLY WITH CHRIST
IN OUR HEAVENLY HOME.

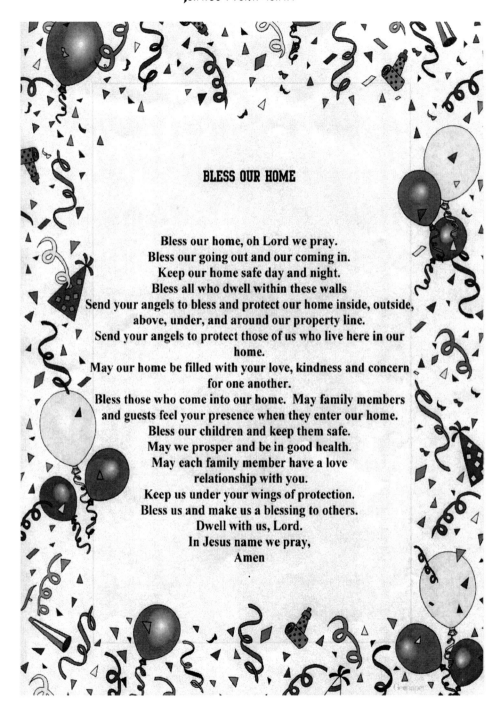

BLESS OUR HOME

Bless our home, oh Lord we pray.
Bless our going out and our coming in.
Keep our home safe day and night.
Bless all who dwell within these walls
Send your angels to bless and protect our home inside, outside,
above, under, and around our property line.
Send your angels to protect those of us who live here in our
home.
May our home be filled with your love, kindness and concern
for one another.
Bless those who come into our home. May family members
and guests feel your presence when they enter our home.
Bless our children and keep them safe.
May we prosper and be in good health.
May each family member have a love
relationship with you.
Keep us under your wings of protection.
Bless us and make us a blessing to others.
Dwell with us, Lord.
In Jesus name we pray,
Amen

MY HUSBAND

May God bless you and allow you to realize how much I love you
and your family loves you.

May God continue to bless you with good health, vigor and
enthusiasm for life.

May God bless you in your sphere of influence. May He radiate
His love through you.

May God bless you with strength and faith so that you will always
be a strong and steady rock in our family.

May God give you the ability to stand for Godly principles and let
your light shine in a darkened world. Matt. 5:16

May God bless you and surround you with His shield of protection.
No weapon formed against you shall prosper. Isaiah 54:17

May God bless you with His plans to prosper you and plans to give
you hope and a future. Jer.29:11

May God bless you with wisdom and understanding so that riches,
honor and long life will be yours. Prov.3:13-16

Janice Fraumann

TO MY WIFE

May the Lord bless you, as His child with:

1. An Open and willing heart to serve Him

2. A loving spirit to your children and husband

3. A discernment to understand those with whom you associate

4. A passion to know God in a deeper and more meaningful way

5. An understanding of His will for your life

6. An abundance of health and prosperity

7. A continued, wonderful relationship with your husband, your children and your grandchildren

8. With joy, happiness and confidence in the future

9. With wisdom and faithful instruction

10. Children who rise and call you blessed and a husband who praises you

11. An ability and energy to bring abundance into the life of your family

12. The ability to be an example of a Godly woman who has an intimate love relationship with God.

SON

May God bless you with the desire to study God's
Word.
May you always know you are loved by God and by me.
May God bless you with protection, good health
and prosperity.
May God bless you with favor among all those with
whom you come in contact.
May God give you the desires of your heart.
May God bless you with wisdom and discernment.
May God bless you with the ability to be a witness
for the Lord and have a ministry to people.
May God bless you with a peaceful spirit that comes
only from God.

With love,

OUR BELOVED DAUGHTER

May God bless you with an abundance of His love
and peace.
May you always know you are loved by God and
by us
May God bless and prosper you in everything you do.
May God give you the desires of your heart.
May God bless those who bless you.
May God bless you with good health,
strength and vitality to
enjoy life and do His will.
May others see the light of God shining
through your life so
that you will be a bright witness for Christ.
May God bless you with a life that will be
a blessed journey
with the Holy Spirit by your side to guide,
teach and comfort you.

With love,

DEAREST GRANDDAUGHTER

I bless you in the name of the Father, Son and
Holy Spirit.
May your days be free from fear, and may you be
blessed with a spirit of power, of love and a
sound mind.
May God bless you with the gift of discernment
to see clearly what is of God.
May God give you the desires of your heart.
May God give you a hunger for His Word.
May God bless everyone who blesses you.
May God give you the ability to focus on the
major goals and aspirations in your life.
May God give you a peace in the middle of the
storms of life.
May God bless you with a special sense of
security to know that I will always love you and
support you in everything you do.
May you know that you are the "light of my life".

1

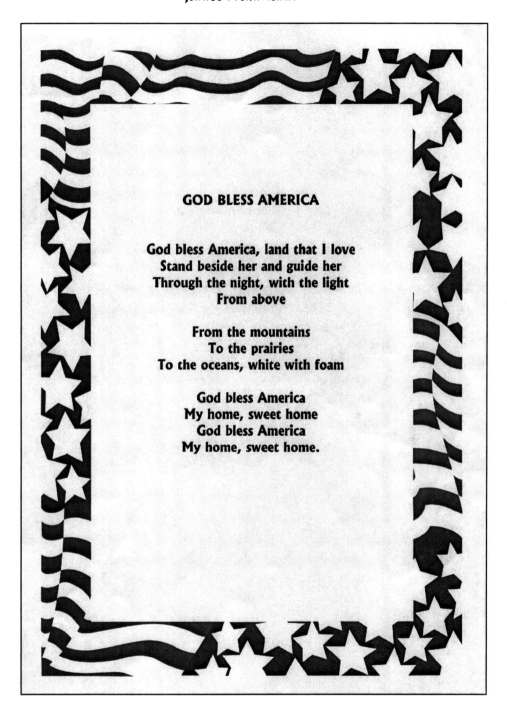

GOD BLESS AMERICA

God bless America, land that I love
Stand beside her and guide her
Through the night, with the light
From above

From the mountains
To the prairies
To the oceans, white with foam

God bless America
My home, sweet home
God bless America
My home, sweet home.

Dearest _____,

I bless you in the name of the Father, Son and
Holy Spirit.
May your days be free from fear, and may you be
blessed with a spirit of power, of love and a
sound mind.
May God bless you with the gift of discernment
to see clearly what is of God.
May God give you a hunger for His Word.
May God bless everyone who blesses you.
May God give you the ability to focus on the
major goals and aspirations in your life.
May God give you a peace in the middle of the
storms of life.
May God bless you with a special sense of
security to know that I will always love you and
support you in everything you do.
May you know you are my 'piece of gold" and the
"light of my life".
May the Lord bless you and keep you;
May the Lord make His face to shine upon you,
and be gracious to you;
May the Lord lift up His countenance upon you,
and give you peace. In the name of Jesus Christ.

SPECIAL BLESSING

MAY GOD BLESS YOU WITH AN UNDERSTANDING THAT YOU ARE THE CHILD OF THE LIVING GOD.

MAY GOD BLESS YOU WITH AN UNDERSTANDING THAT YOUR BODY IS THE TEMPLE OF THE HOLY SPIRIT.

MAY GOD BLESS YOU WITH A DESIRE TO STUDY HIS WORD.

MAY GOD BLESS YOU WITH AN UNDERSTANDING THAT YOU ARE THE LIGHT OF MY LIFE.

THE BEATITUDES

BLESSED ARE THE POOR IN SPIRIT: FOR THEIRS IS THE KINGDOM OF HEAVEN.

BLESSED ARE THEY THAT MOURN: FOR THEY SHALL BE COMFORTED.

BLESSED ARE THE MEEK: FOR THEY SHALL INHERIT THE EARTH.

BLESSED ARE THEY WHICH DO HUNGER AND THIRST AFTER RIGHTEOUSNESS: FOR THEY SHALL BE FILLED

BLESSED ARE THE MERCIFUL: FOR THEY SHALL OBTAIN MERCY.

BLESSED ARE THR PURE IN HEART: FOR THEY SHALL SEE GOD.

BLESSED ARE THE PEACEMAKERS: FOR THEY SHALL BE CALLED THE CHILDREN OF GOD.

BLESSED ARE THEY WHICH ARE PERSECUTED FOR RIGHTEOUSNESS' SAKE: FOR THEIRS IS THE KINGDOM OF HEAVEN.
BLESSED ARE YE WHEN MEN SHALL REVILE YOU, AND PERSECUTE YOU, AND SHALL SAY ALL MANNER OF EVIL AGAINST YOU FALSELY, FOR MY SAKE.

REJOICE, AND BE EXCEEDING GLAD: FOR GREAT IS YOUR REWARD IN HEAVEN: FOR SO PERSECUTED THEY THE PROPHETS WHICH WERE BEFORE YOU.

Grace and Prayer

God is great, God is good
Let us thank Him for our food.
By His hands we are fed.
Give us Lord, our daily bread.

May God bless our family today as we go our separate ways.
May God bless Dad at work.
May God bless Johnny and help him have a good day at school.
May God bless Sarah and help her remember the information for her test.
May God bless me at my job and keep our family under your umbrella of
protection today.

In Jesus name we pray.
Amen

PRAYER OF JABEZ

And Jabez called on the God of Israel saying,

"Oh, that you would bless me indeed,
and enlarge my territory,

that your hand would be with me,

and that you would keep me from evil,

that I may not cause pain."

So God granted him what he requested.

BLESSINGS FOR SHUT-INS

May God give you strength and courage
To face your daily challenges.

May God's richest blessings be upon you
At this thankful time of year
For good health and happiness.

May the peace of God surpass any obstacles or challenges
You are facing at this time.

May the joy of the Lord be your strength
And the Holy Spirit be your comforter.

May the Lord bless you
With an internal peace and comfort.

May God grant you serenity and grace
With a positive outlook for the future.

Trust in the Lord with all your heart
And lean not on your own understanding.

Trust in the Lord with all your heart
For His bounty is plentiful and He
Will sustain you in all your ways.

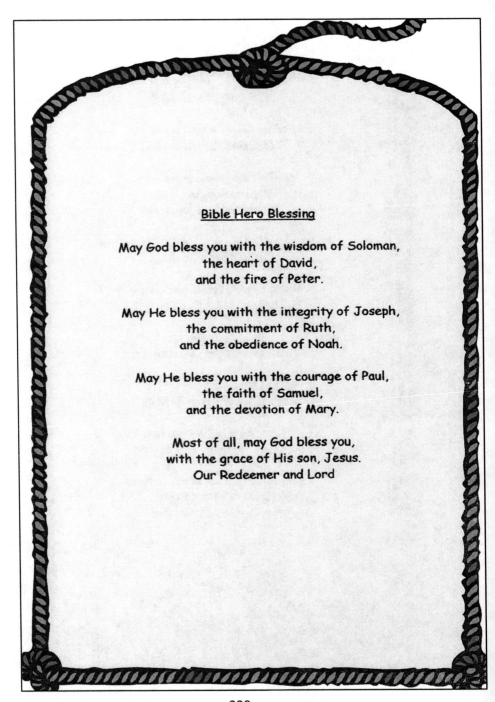

Bible Hero Blessing

May God bless you with the wisdom of Soloman,
the heart of David,
and the fire of Peter.

May He bless you with the integrity of Joseph,
the commitment of Ruth,
and the obedience of Noah.

May He bless you with the courage of Paul,
the faith of Samuel,
and the devotion of Mary.

Most of all, may God bless you,
with the grace of His son, Jesus.
Our Redeemer and Lord

Janice Fraumann

Bedtime Blessing

May God Bless you and keep you through the night.
May he send his angles down to watch over you.

May God's redeeming love encircle you and lift you up
as on the wings of an eagle.

May God's patient, encouraging ways always guide you
and lead you back to his paths of righteousness.

May God's quiet love always be a compass in your life.

May your rest be filled with the dreams of wonder, imagination,
unlimited possibilities, and my love.

In Jesus name.

CPSIA information can be obtained at www.ICGtesting.com
Printed in the USA
LVOW12s0328060614

388879LV00006B/7/P